RULES FOR CHRISTIAN RADICALS

CLIFFORD E WILLIAMS

2

1 JOHN 2:6

"Whoever claims to live in him must walk as Jesus did."

4

TABLE OF CONTENTS

ACKNOWLEDGMENTS 7

PREFACE 9

INTRODUCTION 11

COMPASSION STRUCTURE 19

TWO CLASSES 29

PERSECUTION 43

FAITH 53

RESOLVE 67

HELP 77

PROBLEM ANALYSIS PROCESS 95

FRUIT 107

THE COST 119

PLAN	127
RULES FOR CHRISTIAN RADICALS	135
OPERATION DELUGE	137

ACKNOWLEDGMENTS

I am delivering this work with hope and excitement. My hope is for a wonderful loving church in America. My excitement is that I believe it can happen. This work was paused by great difficulties. At times I thought I wouldn't accomplish the task.

Thanks to my family who are great encouragers. To my deepest and closest friends at World Mission who work tirelessly to deliver the broken and down trodden from despair, I have the greatest respect. I expect to triumph in the cause of Christ, pouring out our lives until we meet our Jesus. Thanks.

PREFACE

Given current social problems, a broken politic in America, and a church that is not living up to its Biblical call, it would be all too easy to tend toward despondency. Around us, formerly stable institutions, like the banking industry, Wall Street, Congress, and the Church, are being discredited. It is a pretty heavy time—many of us are ready to give up caring and just wait for Jesus' return.

The confusion and disillusionment have caused a cynicism that concludes nothing is true and no one can be trusted. There are various schools of thought on how to solve our internal problems in the United States, among them proponents of political change, taxing the rich, smaller class sizes, more social programs, elimination of racism, instituting socialism, or bringing about God's Kingdom on Earth. But I do not think anyone really believes that it is possible to solve the problems of our country, except perhaps a naïve utopist, who is blinded by the light of a vision that has no foundations in natural law. Ideas of the utopian sort are always found to be lacking in practical plausibility, and can be washed away like a sandcastle by the ocean surf. But although a perfect world is unachievable by man, it does not mean that there is nothing to be done! Ultimately, we know that the answer to our nation's problems lies in the hearts of its people. With a deep conviction of personal responsibility toward justice, mercy, and love, we can create a better world.

The change starts first with me, then with you, and then with our friends and families. When I live newly grasped in the hands of formidable love, there is hope for a better nation.

I do not think we can make a perfect world, but I do believe we can change ourselves, and that changing ourselves can help to improve our communities. But what kinds of change should we bring? How do we do it and what will it cost us? What is in it for us, personally? These are all questions that I will deal with in this book. I hope to show you a vision that you have never seen and could not believe possible. Prepare for the next great phase in your life: love without limit.

INTRODUCTION

I write from a desire to see the church mature and be effective. I still believe that we can bring the power back to Main Street. The people who care are frustrated about a variety of problems in the church, but are especially plagued with doubt. Why are we not very effective in changing the world? How can the Christian message produce so little, given the claims of the Bible?

I recently watched a movie called *The Kite Runner*. I hope you watch it, if you haven't already. It's a story of the courage and faithfulness of an Afghan servant boy. The boy and his father were live-in-servants of an influential man in Kabul, Afghanistan. The wealthy man had a son whose only friend was the servant boy. The heart of the servant boy was so inclined toward his friend that, at any request, the servant boy would respond: "For you, a thousand times over."

Together, they shared the sport of what I've dubbed: "kite wars," which is a game where a team of two boys compete with others using their kite as a weapon to cut the strings of the competitors' kite in flight.

The servant boy, who was younger and smaller than his master's son, many times protected his friend against bullies, even though he was often outnumbered and outsized. After a citywide kite competition, the servant boy ran to collect a drifting kite that's string had been cut. Upon catching the kite, he was alone and without his slingshot for defense. Bullies surrounded him like a dark cloud. They told him that if he gave up the rich boy's kite, they would let him go. The brave boy chose not to give up the kite and received the bullies' heinous assault. The rich boy hid nearby and witnessed the assault of his young boy servant.

The wealthy boy's sense of guilt over his friend's assault deteriorated their relationship, and eventually drove him to an irrational deceit. He convinced his father that the servant and his father were unfaithful, and asked that they be fired. And as a result, both father and son were shamed and expelled from their long-time home.

This movie has many lessons to share for viewers. Definitions of courage and cowardice, of faithfulness and deceit are the most obvious. But the movie also introduces the concept of compassion and its relationship to self-protection.

Many of us would not fault the rich boy for his actions. What could he do? The bullies were stronger and outnumbered the two boys. They had previously assaulted the boys, and the rich boy knew there was no hope to satiate their evil intentions. It would accomplish nothing for both of them to be molested. Also, the servant boy could have traded the kite for his own security, so why should the rich boy stand in harm's way because of his friend's outrageous loyalty?

Courage, faithfulness, and compassion are outstanding qualities that are exalted in our culture. But they are costly. Courage can cost you or your family your livelihood, or your lives. In faithfulness, you may sacrifice your rights; with compassion, you may lose more than money. In order to be courageous, faithful, and compassionate we must look at ourselves and acknowledge the truth that virtue requires sacrifice. In order to take courage, be faithful to our call as children of God, and surrender to compassionate living, we must abandon the safety and security that we have built up through a matrix of lies and self-deceit.

The Current State

What can we do to participate in positive change? Life is hectic, after all, and the world seems to be coming apart. We are all working hard to survive, to build families and keep our jobs, to make our spouses happy and enjoy the kids. Some of us are involved in church or civic activities to help make a change, but most people feel overwhelmed by just meeting their personal needs and those of their families.

Add to personal concerns the fact that politics are complex and social problems are huge. The Middle East and the Russians are here to stay, so there goes world peace. The state of the poor continues to decline on an international scale and inner-city crime continues to grow. What can we do to solve such problems?

We can't change the world, but we *can* change. We can become action figures. We can fulfill the imagined life of extraordinary love.

But what if we wanted to change, what if we wanted to help people and were bold enough to hope? If we were sufficiently brave to act on behalf of others. Where would we start? How would we do it? How do we get the most out of our lives?

What It Will Look Like

We can't heal all the sick, feed all the poor, and solve all the mental illness, but we can care for those around us who need help.

I can serve the sick, and I can feed the poor that I come to know. I am not equipped to heal mental illness, but perhaps I could console them and be patient with them to give them hope and support.

What if only 25% of my church body began to take personal responsibility for the homeless who wanted to move forward? Some could sell their homes in the suburbs and move with others to a struggling neighborhood to serve.

It would not only help those in need, but establish our witness. Your family, friends, and co-workers, non-Christian and Christian, will notice a difference in the good lifestyle you live, exemplified in a manifestation of this Jesus lifestyle.

How We Can Do It

We are not helpless, although it is convenient to think so. It doesn't cost much to resolve that the world's problems are too complex and sigh as if we really intended to do anything more than wring our hands. If we intend to make change, we must have a personal transformation, a transformation that extends to our family and church. With a clear strategy for each, we will see reformation.

The change I'm talking about is that we engage the world, not that we agree that everything will get better.

The reformation is orderly: first me, then the closest to me...and if it goes beyond that, great. If not, I am doing my part.

In order to make the alteration, we first must attain a firm understanding of God's plan, His priorities, and how He wants to use us. When we understand that He wants to have us live a sacrificial life of love, we must figure out how to do it.

You must go to where the people are who need help. We must get close enough to people's lives that we can see their need and act. If you are a typical, middle class person, you don't know poor people. When you discover them, you'll find that to help them the cost is blood, sweat, and tears.

Many times we are afraid to help because of the potential personal loss. At other times, we are fearful of persecution. It takes a deep trust in Christ to overcome such fears.

Determination derived from conviction will push us to continue, even as we are suffering from loss. But, the change cannot be made alone. We will need help and encouragement to continue and produce the results we desire. Joining a community such as operationdeluge.com, which hosts a network of Christians around the country who are working hard to make this a better world, will provide ideas and encouragement to carry out God's plan.

The desired outcome is to be obedient to Christ and to bring His will on Earth as it is in Heaven, which we can do only if we personalize His will and act. Make a personal plan to be in the right place to help others and ensure that you have a systemized plan of encouragement.

This book is about providing solutions. With it, we will make a plan for personal change to accomplish transformation. To attain this renovation, we will need what the poor Afghan boy from *The Kite Runner* has: faithfulness to protect a friend, courage to take on the bullies, compassion to protect the weak, and willingness to suffer for love.

13

THE COMPASSION STRUCTURE

A new picture of compassion is needed, but ripping-up an old concept is tough. Rethinking the treasured masterpiece is hard; we are accustomed to its unquestioned beauty. We assume its legitimacy and are reluctant to authenticate it.

The general understanding of compassion is like an uncomfortable suit that is rarely worn. Like a suit, it is brought out for special occasions—funerals and weddings, for example. Otherwise, we rarely need it. So rarely is it used that it looks strange in the mirror as we pose in it—rigid, uncomfortable, and constricting. But we wear it anyway, as we are expected to. It helps us feel good about ourselves and gives a respectable image. But, the truth is that we are happy to take it off. Just like the suit, compassion is removed after the funeral. We fold it up and pack it carefully away for the next reluctant, but necessary, display.

And why should we do anything else? Compassion is not needed to get by, is it? It doesn't feed or clothe us. It won't get you a job. Most often, it's used as a tool, an ornament to benevolent speech or to embellish talk driven by moral outrage in favor of the underprivileged.

Like an ornament, it's great to admire from a distance, such as we admire the lives of dead saints. But what has compassion ever done for us?

Compassion for others might never have brought you more than a vague sense of relief from guilt. But when you are in need of compassion, it is another story entirely.

When you need compassion, it feels like the life raft that keeps you from drowning. Unfortunately, it is harder to find compassion than to find a volunteer to serve at a leper colony. Even if someone notices your need and puts on their suit of compassion, it is only a motionless sympathy. And sympathy won't pay your electric bill.

Compassion is misused and misunderstood, like so many other virtues. Each definition of the word compassion recognizes suffering and the desire to help those who are suffering. Bible references often show action following compassion. The story of the Good Samaritan is the most referenced, as is the parable of Matthew 25:40: "I tell you the truth, whatever you did for one of the least of these brothers of mine, you did for me."

The desire to take action distinguishes compassion from simple emotion. Sympathy is a friendly acquaintance, but compassion is a mother. Sadness is a stranger's stare and head shake, but compassion stoops down to embrace my helpless state. In the same way, compassion, not sympathy, fulfills the Great Command.

God's mandate is that you love your neighbor as yourself. Christ demonstrated this mandate in His life, and we all know the Golden Rule: "Do unto others as you would have them do unto you." But though we all know it, why is the world in chaos? Where's the love? Is the world as it is just because it lies in the hands of bad people? I propose that the current state is not the fault of bad people. Rather, it is the fault of the "moral" majority, who have stood by and done nothing. Those who know better should *do* better.

Wrecking Time

A poor foundation has been laid for compassion. The concrete, the rebar, and all the components were hardened together, but the foundation has not been laid on Christ. We call him Savior and Lord, but we reform Him, His mission, and His purpose to our preferences. That is why society is cracking and ready to collapse on our heads. On one hand we say to God, "I have given you my life." And yet still we use our lives on ourselves.

Many think that evangelism is the most important action a Christian can perform. This is an understandable assumption, since people who die without Jesus will go to Hell. Helping them find the path to salvation seems to be the most compassionate thing a Christian can do. Evangelism is a vital part of God's plan, but it is like cement—it cannot be laid without the proper framework in place. Evangelism is not our leading edge, and it isn't the most important action. Imaging Jesus is first.

Christ is to be emulated; we should live to be like him in the world. Christ cared for people. If they needed food, he fed them. If they wanted wine, he made it. He served tirelessly, walked miles to reach those in need, stepped out of Heaven into a corrupt world, and even died on a cross for crimes he never committed—all for our sakes. Modern day Christians talk and do nothing, and we are seen as a bunch of priggish, self-righteous know-it-alls. He *showed* people the love He commanded, and it changed them.

It is easy to believe that we could never attain Christ's lifestyle. But does that mean we should not try? Is it due worship to hold him separate from ourselves? Or is it cowardice—laziness? We seem to enjoy the convenient, hopeless state of being "only human." It scares me, this all-too-comfortable repose. We settle into the habit of Christian language, tithes, and church attendance. And then we go about our lives. Yet, in spite of our conjured difficulty with Christ and certainty that we can't be like Him, He calls, "Come follow me." He won't let us plant

Him as an idyllic bobble-head on our dashboard to be irreverently admired. The highest form of praise, after all, is emulation. You will worship Him by copying Him!

I propose we look at the heart of Christ in order to understand how to be like Him. The desire of Jesus was to please God the Father. He pleased the Father in all He has done. His worship was from the heart, as demonstrated by His devotion to love. He had great expectation in prayer and His friendships were sincere. He fought for the truth, opposed those who pretended love, touched the leper, and reformed the reviled prostitute. But how do we do the same?

Building

What if Safeway was a place to encounter the community? What about downtown? We often walk by God inspired moments without taking a second glance. When you see a guy struggling in a walker or a person digging for change in a grocery line, do you consider them a foolish nuisance to your tight schedule? Instead, think of them as opportunities for you to act and help according to Christ's message. Rather than ignoring those who might benefit from your help, listen, talk, ask, and interact with them...you might learn that their problems are something you can help.

Imagine what your life would be if you moved to a poor neighborhood. How would you interact to influence and help that community? What would your friends say? Your family and co-workers would be shocked. Think about it! How would such a move affect your witness?

It doesn't matter where you begin. You could assist a team that feeds the poor. You could help at a crisis pregnancy office. It is only imperative that you begin somewhere. Doing nothing is foolish and sinful.

Every day is an adventure, filled with opportunities, if you are looking for them. You might ride the bus, just to find opportunities to help others. How else will you know the need, if you are not a witness to it? We are to be like Jesus, not simply "good" people. Good people are everywhere, but the Christian has a duty beyond himself. We are people of faith and compassion.

You must serve. After all, who is the greatest in God's eyes? Not theologians or pastors, but those who serve the most. And we are always on duty—love doesn't take a break. Jesus wasn't on a ministry time-table, serving his fellow man from 9 am to 5 pm with the weekends off. But pastors, elders, and pew-sitters are comfortable living down to this standard.

Here is an example of what your witness could look like. You decide to serve at an organization that feeds the homeless. By hanging out, helping, and visiting, you begin to learn more about those you are helping. While you are counseling a guy, a person who is served by the organization (Jon) asks for a ride to a nearby town for court, and you accept. As you drive Jon to court the next day, he tells you why he is in trouble, and you discover that he isn't receiving good representation from the public defender. Jon also mentions that his estranged wife takes care of the kids and that she is having problems with her car. After dropping him off at court, you stop by and meet his wife and look at the car. You are not good with cars, so you call a fellow Christian who works as a mechanic and schedule him to look at the car that Saturday.

On Saturday, your wife goes with you and meets Jon's wife, Lisa, and their three kids. While you and your friend work on the car with Jon, the ladies visit. Your friend brings along his cousin Mike to help. He is not a Christian, but you have a chance to show the gospel to him. Meanwhile, a neighbor drops by and mentions that he just lost his job.

It just keeps going.

In a short time, you have fed some people, provided counseling, transported Jon to court, made a new friend, learned more about the judicial system, realized where the system needs improving, and bore witness to Christ. Your Christian buddy is helping you serve others. Your wife is providing emotional support for Lisa and the kids. You have intertwined your life with the lives of others to serve, care, and evangelize. This is how it happens. Your ministry is people!

Caring for people is your ministry. Love is Christ's command. That is why we should just put ourselves in the right environment and be open to say, "Yes" to the needs of others! There is no special training needed to follow Christ. Just say, "Yes."

There is one more important thing to note. When co-workers, friends, and family ask about what you have been doing lately, you'll have a great story to tell. This might seem self-aggrandizing, but the stories you tell about your life do more than entertain—they are part of your obedience to God. That is why Jesus said, "In the same way, let your light shine before men, that they may see your good deeds and praise your Father in heaven."[1]

From this platform, you can emphasize to others how possible it is to live a Christ-lifestyle. You can show them that the ways of Christ are a human lifestyle, that they are salvation and repentance all in one—the will of God acted out before the world. You will show that this lifestyle is the substance of faith and a true example of Christ's love.

---

[1] Matt 5:16

Conclusion

Humanity's needs are great, but you can help to serve them. We are all Jesus to the world. We begin by helping people as we would want them to help us. This help does not require a large budget or ministry plan. Christ's love continues from moment to moment and circumstance to circumstance.

Like the shining of the sun, God's love never ceases. Those who are His are always giving and caring. We are eager, always saying, "Yes." Christians are driven to act on behalf of the needs of others.

Jesus our LORD says in Luke 6:32–36,

> If you love those who love you, what credit is that to you? Even "sinners" love those who love them. And if you do good to those who are good to you, what credit is that to you? Even "sinners" do that. And if you lend to those from whom you expect repayment, what credit is that to you? Even "sinners" lend to "sinners," expecting to be repaid in full. But love your enemies, do good to them, and lend to them without expecting to get anything back. Then your reward will be great, and you will be sons of the Most High, because he is kind to the ungrateful and

wicked. Be merciful, just as your Father is merciful.

If you think what you have just read is real New Testament living, wait until you get noticed. Yes, you are venturing into a new realm.

TWO CLASSES

A plan to act on behalf of others must recognize that helping those in need is a complex and messy undertaking. Our strategy must understand those in our culture, so we can work amongst them in a culturally appropriate way. We must work with those in trouble while living in a neighborhood, interacting with co-workers, sharing life with family, and participating in other voluntary associations. We aren't simply helping those in difficulties but attempting to influence our community in a positive way. We would like others to change and view themselves as their brothers' keepers. With a clear understanding of each group, we can formulate a strategic plan that will effectively maximize our influence for Christ's sake.

I wish that Christianity could live up to the mistakenly clean image formed by the many antiseptic, germ-free sermons we've heard. This image has been reinforced in books and Christian radio. It is of the Christian who is smiling, who is neat, who is "square."

I understand why our religion is presented like this. We are endeavoring to illustrate a wholesome propaganda, an image that is worthy of God. Great! There is nothing wrong with having a well-ordered life or with avoiding the influence of pop-cultures. There is nothing wrong with avoiding bad company. Christians should be wholesome and unsullied as we engage in our culture to fulfill God's ultimate plan.

A sanitized version of our religion may be preferable, but it should not fog the view of our purpose! The image of the smiling, tidy, respectable Christian can hinder the advancement of a compassionate lifestyle in the real world. If we continue to foster this image without understanding why Jesus healed us, we will not fulfill his expressed goal to love the world through us.

Our true purpose is to engage with a world that isn't tidy. It is chaotic and confused, dirty and profane. Thus, a Christian in the course of Christ's mission is not engaged in the maintenance of his own sparkling clean image, but soils himself in the pursuit of bringing a better life to others. As we engage in the community to help others, our adored image of purity and pristine reputation must fall away.

We have to deal with complex situations. Drunks, broken families, unsustainable visions of the world, and sex offenders all provide us with grave challenges. There are no simple and manufactured answers to help us solve the complex equations that hinder the lives of those whom you would help.

For example, when you are helping a selfish drug user to advance his life, a sex offender to get a job, or a homeless mom with kids to create a steady home for her family, countless problems present themselves.

My wife and I were once helping a young man in his early twenties. As a pre-teen, he had been found guilty of a sex offense. He spent most of the next ten years in juvenile detention and went on to spend time in prison. He came to our house with a grim spirit, dressed in punk attire and makeup. He had given up hope although he did not despair—he carried with him an "I don't give a shit!" attitude. He couldn't get a job because he was still required to register as a sex-offender (SO). He had nothing but a bag of clothes in his possession. He was a pagan and performed pagan rituals, even though his father was a follower of Jesus.

We wondered what we could do to help him. Should we help him get a job? Should we bring him to church and small group with us, or should we just talk to him about the love of Jesus?

We began by getting a general understanding of where he was coming from. Given his drug use, we decided to allow him to stay on the farm rather than forcing him to get a job. Because the message of Jesus had been pounded into the young man for years, we didn't require him to go to church or small group. We thought that it would exacerbate his hostility to Christ and the Church. Additionally, I didn't talk to him about the love of Christ.

In time, we got the court to drop his SO status so he no longer had to register. We are working to have his juvenile record sealed. We got him a job and, eventually, a place to live.

This whole process took a year and a half. We had to help convince the court that he was reformed and had been doing well. We had to convince potential employers to take a chance to hire him. It was so hard to find someone who would rent to a sex offender that it took almost four months to find him a place to live.

He was always looking for an argument, until eventually I asked him to quit talking to me about the church and Christ. His aggression toward Christianity was such that it wasn't possible to have a reasonable discussion without further engraining his bias. Still, he eventually came to Christ, although we never tried to convince him to and didn't invite him to church functions.

Once he began to see the opportunities before him, his attitude dramatically changed and he began to hope. The makeup, which was a symbol of despair and rebellion, disappeared from his face. He didn't need it any more. I would like to say that he lived happily ever after, but then who does? He is still having difficulty finding his path in life and needs to develop a lot in order to find more successful ways to engage with his world. He is still working on resolving conflict, taking personal responsibility, and fostering an enduring attitude to finish what he has begun.

Middle class people and the poor approach life in different ways. They have different world views and self-perceptions. Street people evoke in others many prejudices, stereotypes, and unreasoned empathies, but none of these can touch the complexity of the issues experienced in the real lives of these people. Our stereotypes of street people obscure our vision of the true situation. It may be assumed that those on the street have had difficult lives, haven't been loved, want a home, just need an opportunity, are criminals, and don't know about Jesus. I would ditch all of these assumptions.

I've worked with hundreds of people who were homeless and in need of help, and each one has his own complex set of circumstances. Using a template for "understanding" can only help so far. I have spoken to young adult street workers in Portland, and the kids were not generally from poor families but upper-middle class. How do you help someone who could just ask his parents, but chooses not to? Until you actively involve yourself in solving the unique problems that surround the individual, you can't know how to work through these difficulties.

Another issue is how to deal with the person you would help when he is in your environment. If you have someone at your house, for example, do you keep your kids away in order to protect them? If you do, it may result in an attitude detrimental to compassion, an inadvertent admission to your children that such people are dangerous and should be avoided. Should you instead include the individual in family events—should you embrace them and help them so they can find belonging? The reality of polluting your family is real if you let this person become a part of it. The benefits of including the individual and the development of compassionate convictions for family and community are immense, but there is a risk!

We've adopted three children in an effort to help improve lives. Two of these children have educational difficulties and another is in trouble with the law. We face many complex situations as a family. When we did foster care for our second adopted son, we had to follow the state's regulations on care, which also created some difficult situations. We had to choose between doing what was right for the child at the risk of facing the heavy hand of the state and submitting to the state's law and hurting the child.

Thus you begin to see why helping the less fortunate can be a messy business. You are faced with many damned-if-you-do and damned-if-you-don't choices. Some people are helped and some get hurt. It isn't like the movies, where everything always turns out for the best. In the movies, the outcome is manipulated by the writer. The reality is far more likely to end in failure.

Real life isn't clean. We know this from experience; we know this from reading the Bible. People get hurt and suffer, even when they are trying to do the right thing. Life is complex, and the "correct" mode is not always the easy one. In some cases, any plan of action still leaves collateral damage.

Given these realities, we need a few more pieces of information to fully develop a true context for a viable plan for compassionate living and influencing the people of our world.

Background

Let me give a framework by which we can understand the people around us. The poor, the working middle class, small business owners, professionals, and the wealthy all have particular biases, gifts, blind spots, and unchallenged assumptions. For instance, many poor people understand the criminal justice system better than most rich and middle class people do. Why is that, do you think? It is because of the relatively high crime rate amongst them.

Have you ever heard of a "public pretender"? This is a diminutive term used by those accused of a crime to indicate that their public defender doesn't really care about them or their case. Some public defenders seem to lack energy, and negative outcomes occur for their clients as a result. In many cases, such a lawyer uses his easiest tool to bring a case to an end, and negotiates with the prosecuting attorney for a plea bargain rather than working hard to present a solid case. Then, the "public pretender" warns the client that if they do not take the plea, they could get even more time on their sentence. Such a lawyer doesn't fight to defend his client. It seems to the accused that the lawyer shirks his work and is well paid for it by the state.

Most crimes are committed by and against impoverished people. A crime history can also be a cause of poverty. On the other hand, well-off or middle class people who generally have minor problems, who have steady work and care for their families, assume that their lives are so successful because they are good people. They are approved by their peers and are therefore satisfied. These differences in lifestyles cause great differences in understanding. Both those in trouble and those helping need to learn about the true state of the world and make changes from there.

This is how it works. You meet a guy on the street who is unemployed. Some say, "Just go get a job." But finding a job is harder than it sounds even for an educated and experienced professional—how much more so it is for the homeless! They are dirty from living on the street. They do not have an address, a phone number, or even an alarm clock. If they have a resume, which is unlikely, they do not have much of a work history. Many suffer from addiction to drugs or alcohol, and thus exhibit negative attitudes, poor self-image, and emotional distress. In a competitive market, where employers can have their pick of hundreds of applicants, why would anyone hire such a vagrant?

If you want to help this guy on the street, you start by learning how he thinks the world works and develop solutions that empathize with his experience but still work to extract him from the mess and elevate him to a new standard of living. An economic improvement will be the result, but it is not the whole goal. More importantly, the work must restore the man's self respect and dignity. It needs to be communicated that he can make changes to his life and maintain a different lifestyle from the one he is used to, until he is no longer dependent but sees himself as able bodied. Thus, before "getting a job," you have to help him create a proper context for living, as well as the methods and strategies to navigate this new way of life.

Teaching in this context happens in the course of daily life with the individual, as opportunities arise, in much the same was as we teach our children. If it the situation requires, you must teach them to clean their rooms, be sensible, and speak politely. When they throw a fit or act irresponsibly, it is your responsibility to correct them. You give vision and hope and encouragement. If you are a parent or have lived in a stable family, much of this is second nature. The difference is that sometimes the individuals are your peers or even older.

Correcting adults can be dicey—I don't want to get your hopes up. Most mature adults do not take correction. With an immature and rebellious adult, teaching is even harder. The best tactic to reach your goal of changing someone's behavior is through communication. Be direct and unemotional. Outline that the change is achievable and that it would benefit him or her. Also, focus on the major issues. Do not nitpick. It would drive you crazy to have a priggish, overbearing overlord watching and criticizing your every move, and the person you are trying to help will not feel differently. Maintain a relationship that is trusting and positive, so the adult will know that you have his or her best interests at heart.

It is not well known that God specially gifts these underprivileged. I've addressed the gospel to many people, and I've generally found that, as the scriptures state, it is difficult for a rich man to be saved. Those who are well off assume that, because they are good and relatively astute, they are good enough for Jesus. Thus it says in James 2:5, "Listen, my dear brothers: Has not God chosen those who are poor in the eyes of the world to be rich in faith and to inherit the kingdom he promised to those who love him?" This gift of faith is still possible to the self-made person, but more difficult.

The gift to the poor is faith. I believe that rich people are more likely than the poor to be lacking when it comes to faith. Perhaps it is because the rich man's view of himself and others like him is one of self-approval, due to the reinforcement of culture values. People of means feel good about themselves as a result of how others see them. They assume without thought or reason that God approves of them as well, and do not question that He may not. This misguided assumption is damning to the rich. Being good in one's own eyes is not enough—God's ways are higher than and different from our own.

Conversely, the poor are constantly subjected to a reflected image provided by society and media that depicts them as low creatures. Because their society thinks so little of them, they may feel estranged from God. They have a harder time believing they are "good" people, because society doesn't see them that way. As a result, they are more aware of their need for God. They do not need to be convinced that they need His forgiveness.

The way in which we deal with the neediest of our neighborhoods will determine whether we are able to break the lie that the self-approved live in. We need to reform as much as they do, or else we will simply be blind guides. It should humble us to know that we are all the same in God's eyes, except that those who have more have a greater responsibility to use our advantages to lift up those who have less.

Thus there is another reason to pursue the improved well-being of others: enlightenment. Through helping others, we will see ourselves and our culture more clearly.

This enlightenment will then provide us the opportunity to help our middle class brothers. Your revelations will open a vista for the self-satisfied. They will see the difference between their lives and the mission laid out by Christ. They will be forced to consider whether they are merciful to wicked and ungrateful wretches, as Jesus was, whether they care for their enemies, whether they can turn the other cheek. When they see you operating in Christ' reality, when they see you perform, they will receive the Holy Spirit's conviction. They will notice that their reasons for not helping feel less and less comfortable. And they will begin a mental war of self-justification and doubt. We all know this war. You ask yourself, "Am I helping? Do I love? What am I sacrificing? Do I care? Am I really a good person?"

What questions, when the scripture is clear on this point! As in Jer 22:16, which reads, "He defended the cause of the poor and needy, and so all went well. Is that not what it means to know me?" According to these words, helping those in need is necessary in order to know God, which shouldn't surprise you. If you recall, the bottom line for Jesus' rebuke of the religious leaders of His time was their lack of compassion. That is why Matt 23:23–24 records Him as saying:

> Woe to you, teachers of the law and Pharisees, you hypocrites! You give a tenth of your spices—mint, dill and cumin. But you have neglected the more important matters of the law—*justice, mercy and faithfulness*. You should have practiced the latter, without neglecting the former. You blind guides! You strain out a gnat but swallow a camel.
> [Emphasis added.]

But you might say: This applies to the Pharisee, not to me!

It applies if it applies.

Are you good at being there for your church but do not take the time to be there for your fellow man? If so, take heed that the shoe may fit you. You complain, "But I'm saved." If you were truly saved, you would love God and do what he said. This is sour medicine, but it will heal you. It will set you free.

Many people have interlocked their lives with the lower, middle, and upper classes of society in an organic witness to the holy lifestyle. This gives them the power of the Holy Spirit. Through this new life, He gives insight, and you gain clout because you create experiences and have wisdom to share. You will develop a way of articulating this insight that propels others to action, conviction, or repentance. Perhaps you will inspire them to a new way of living that follows the teachings of Jesus. This inspiration can benefit not only your unsaved friends, but your church also.

Once we have had our eyes opened, we need a viable plan through which we will lift up others. A new perspective is the necessary foundation, but after it is built we must carry on in the new way to build an active, compassionate plan of action.

PERSECUTION

"There is no persecution in the United States."

I have heard this said often. I know what Christians mean when they say this. Relative to what is suffered in China, other communist countries, and Islamic states, they are right that we suffer nothing. But of course, there have been religious martyrs in the U.S., and others have died for the sake of social justice. An innumerable number of people have suffered in various ways, but we hardly hear about it or see it today in the U.S. In Islamic states and in Communist countries it is rampant, but not here.

Persecution can come in various forms. Employment, social acceptance, and business opportunities can be restricted because of the activities you engage in that are outside of the cultural norms. People suffer for dressing strangely or engaging in activities on the cultural fringe. But, people rarely suffer in the U.S. for doing good.

Why, then, do we not see persecution? Let's reason together. Since there are always opportunities to do good, we should never lack opportunities to suffer. Therefore, seeing as we never lack the problems of poverty and injustice, we can only conclude that there should be many stories in our local neighborhood of good people suffering because they have done good. Since we do not see such suffering, we can reasonably conclude that there aren't many noble people amongst us.

My wife received a call some time ago. The individual railed at her for housing a sex offender. He accused her of an act of evil. I do not know where he expects them to go. It was so upsetting for her to be accused of evil when doing good, to feel unsupported by her community in her attempts to follow the command of God.

I recently spoke to a Christian friend whom I've known for a few years. When I told him about the strange scrutiny I was under for the work I had undertaken and my subsequent trouble with the neighbors, community, and public officials, he said, "That's why people don't get involved!" Most people are way too sensible to create these kinds of problems for themselves. They are careful to march in step with culture's hordes. They avoid the trouble that comes with doing what is good.

The Source

For the sake of good, for the sake of Christ, you may act against the cultural norms of your society. If you adopt a foster child, if you live well under your financial potential in order to dedicate yourself to the service of the poor, if drug users frequent your house because you befriended them, what would your neighbors think? How would you explain the frequent visits of police to your house?

In the eyes of your peers, your activities would seem irresponsible.

Today I received a call from a young mother who has nowhere to go. She and her child are recently under the scrutiny of CPS. Now that she is to be homeless, she will have her child taken from her. At our house, we have a complex situation of housing two toddlers who belong to another family we have helped. If we invited the young mother and her child into our home, we would be in danger of CPS's scrutiny. They have a litany of requirements that outlines, among other things, how many people can be living in your home. It is a strange situation when the state makes it dangerous for a family to help someone in need. You would never know these dilemmas if you weren't involved, and so it can be easy to conclude there isn't persecution. But you would be wrong.

Your culture and family say that it is reasonable to help others as long as you do not put yourself in jeopardy. I stand to point out the hypocrisy of this systematic flaw. It states that it is only acceptable to exhibit caring behavior if you will be repaid with notoriety, money, or affection, or if doing so won't cause suffering to you and your family. Do you see if there is a cultural pat on the back or a financial gain to helping others, then it makes sense to them. But if you choose to limit your future or your family's potential in order to help others, they will say that you have taken your religion too far. And yet these same people would exalt those who have joined the military for taking a risk at great expense in order to provide security for their families. Does anyone shoot them down? No, because we personally gain for their sacrifice and service. In fact, we commend them. What a blatant blindness.

So the excuses, the inventions of reasons to avoid the trouble of helping others abound. The list rises tall like a mountain, and the pressure from society to fall in line can seem excruciating. It brings to mind the horrible scene from *1984,* where Orwell's protagonist, Winston, screams "Do it to Julia!" when under torture to fall in line with his society's norm.

Family, friends, community, church, and government can be a great source of comfort, security, and strength. They can provide for our health and welfare. But there are forbidden acts that can cause these pillars of strength to fall on us—to introduce tension, ridicule, or even banishment upon us.

Mothers and fathers want to be proud of their children. They want them to have good families and prosperity. If their children are well, parents are proud. Communities and churches, meanwhile, want harmony and safety. And government is in place to ensure these. But, if we choose to help a homeless man and he lives at our house, our relatives might feel uncomfortable. Our parents might feel that we are harming our welfare and that of our children, and put pressure on us to end this arrangement. Our neighbors might fear for the safety of their families. For example, I have a friend whose relatives would not allow him over for the holidays because he was to bring with him a friend. This friend committed a sex crime when he was less than 18 years old. You may say that you empathize and I say, "You white washed tomb!" Has this individual committed the unforgivable sin? Who made us judge?

Community and churches respond the same. In my community, rumors fly because my family helps people. Public officials frequently visit our house as part of the process of our helping, and thus false reports have circulated that required Child Protective Services to investigate our home. More than one Christian family has chosen to reject our company because we help the unseemly. We touch the leper, and are made unclean.

But according to Matt 5:10–16, Jesus has predicted such troubles and asserts that they are worth it!

> Blessed are those who are persecuted because of righteousness, for theirs is the kingdom of heaven. Blessed are you when people insult you, persecute you and falsely say all kinds of evil against you because of me. Rejoice and be glad, because great is your reward in heaven, for in the same way they persecuted the prophets who were before you.

And in Luke 6:22–23, he reasserts, "Blessed are you when men hate you, when they exclude you and insult you and reject your name as evil, because of the Son of Man. Rejoice in that day and leap for joy, because great is your reward in heaven. For that is how their fathers treated the prophets."

Apostle Paul writes in 2 Tim 3:12, "In fact, everyone who wants to live a godly life in Christ Jesus will be persecuted."

There seems to be so little persecution in the U.S.—perhaps it is because there are few Godly people. If there were many, wouldn't there be a great deal more notable discrimination? The only discrimination I've seen is of the Christian message, but not much of Christian action.

Why does difficulty follow doing what is right? There are various reasons: envy, loss of money, loss of prestige, loss of power, loss of business, loss of love, loss of self-esteem, pressure to change, and misunderstanding. When is "right" is upheld, oppressors and even those amongst us are offended. Friends, family, and church members might judge you as an evil doer. They will fight to keep things as they are, and any excuse to maintain the status quo will suffice.

I've read about the difficulties faced by William and Catherine Booth, the founders of the Salvation Army. Through their work, they convinced many people to quit drinking. Local bar owners were being put out of business, as a result. After some time, groups were formed to throw vegetables and bricks at Booth's followers. Many died of blunt trauma, all for righteousness's sake.

Richard Wurmbrand, a Romanian pastor in the mid-1900s, suffered with his co-laborers under the communists. He spent fourteen years in prison along with many others, proclaiming freedom from sin. They suffered not for their "faith," but for their action. They held secret church meetings and evangelized when it was against the law. And what of the famous and admired Corrie ten Boom, who with her family in the Netherlands hid Jews from the Nazi regime only to suffer shame, imprisonment, loss of property, and death? But these people were the exception, not the rule, and all were in Christian Nations that were saturated with people like you and me, all who should have been acting the same. "But small is the gate and narrow the road that leads to life, and only a few find it."[2] Heroism, selflessness, risk taking, self-sacrifice, and determination are culturally honored. They are depicted in movies like *Gladiator*, *300*, *Robin Hood*, and *Braveheart*. But these characteristics are not honored socially, among one another. Instead, we have relegated these qualities to super-heroes, and insist that it is not up to us to be heroes.

Christ calls men and women to be super-men and -women. And why not? We have the power of God, who raises the dead, living in us.

A youth worker once challenged a junior high group I was helping with the words, "Don't you think God can change things?" He was talking about changing things at school. We shrank back in shame, knowing that he was right. We had thought God wouldn't help, not necessarily that he couldn't. But twenty years have passed, and things have grown worse. God didn't change the world, and the situation is only getting worse because we do not act.

---

[2] Matt 7:14

I do not question Jesus or His Spirit, but only those who claim they know Him and yet do nothing.

According to Eschatologists, when the "love of many grow cold" it shows that the end is near. This is what is prophesied. But that is no reason to despair. The cause is the coldness, as prophesied, which brings about the End. We get cold and he comes—not he makes us cold and then He comes.

FAITH

I am tired of people making so much out of this idea of faith. It has been made so mysterious. Light a candle, squint your eyes tight and say this prayer, believe it will happen, profess it...and it will come to pass. Sounds kind of conjured, almost witch crafty, huh? Except that faith isn't so mysterious. It is more like, "I believe, therefore I act." When this is the case, I can see the result of my faith. It brings me hope and peace. Through it, I can be happy even without possessing the goal of my faith. In addition, without this trust you cannot obey Jesus. You cannot persevere unless you trust Him and know what He wants.

Remember waiting for Christmas when you were young? Just the mention of it reminded you of the mystery and hope. When you grabbed an old catalog, you would look through all the pictures of what you would like to receive, even as early as July. In the same way, we use our mind with our faith. We can be distant from what we pray and hope for, but just thinking about its result can make us tremble with excitement.

This faith driven hope empowers us. It moves us to continue and work. You can enjoy the distance prize in a moment of discouragement and pain. It pulls you to obey because of the prize of eternal life. It is ours through Jesus, so we continue to labor as He did for the love of God and His pleasure for the benefit of the world.

I've visited quite a few people to discuss the issue of the Sermon on the Mount. I've been challenged by His words and encourage people to consider them carefully. The Sermon describes the life of faith, which is synonymous with the life of Jesus. Many good non-Christian people have told me that they could live as described in His sermon, that they could turn the other cheek, go the extra mile, and so on, and that they could do so without Jesus. This assertion seems possible when you first hear it. The people who say so really believe that they can, but they are kidding themselves. They have not thought about it thoroughly or been put to the test. What about when it hurts? What happens when the people you're helping are unkind, steal from you, disrespect you? When obeying is agony, it becomes very hard to continue. If there is no benefit or reason that is as large as God's plan and the goal of eternal life it cannot be done. Since Jesus has authority to provide what He promises we can follow through, even under duress. Persevering through pain and difficulty is what separates sheep from goats.

Time and pain push us to give up our obedience. We want to take it easy, to repose. Serene bliss is what we really want, not a cross. I've explained without an argument that when it starts to hurt or "not work," we quit. This is well understood. We will not continue to obey if the pain continues. Without exception, we begin looking for release, for an easy way out. This is where faith begins. This is ultimately why we need it. This is when it shows its power.

As I write this, I'm scaring myself. I see the potential cost. I realize God can take us to many situations that are beyond our natural abilities and can be very costly. I can imagine some crazy, scary scenarios. I remember telling my little brother and sister horror stories when we were kids. However, I think I was the only one of us who was afraid and couldn't sleep, afterwards. I hope I'm not the only one who understands that faith is very challenging.

God is doing serious work, which requires that we give Him a deep kind of trust. The only way to please Him is by this trust: "And without faith it is impossible to please God."[3]

Another scripture states, "Everything that does not come from faith is sin."[4]

---

[3] Heb 11:6
[4] Rom 14:23

That you need faith is obvious, but what are the tools of faith? How do we encourage ourselves and others when under duress?

It is vital that you know and understand the following in order to keep your faith strong:

1. God is here now.
2. He told me in the Word.
3. He has shown me.
4. He is in control.
5. I can see it.
6. I do not care what it costs.
7. He will not forsake me.

And in order to make real change in the world, you must be willing to be decisive and to never look back.

These are not just things to know on a superficial level—you need to train yourself. Without practice, obeying and perseverance can be a struggle. You must make time to practice your faith. Set time aside, just as you would to improve any skill. You need to prepare yourself, because the time is coming when you'll need them; the worst time to learn how to shoot your weapon is in the midst of battle.

God is Here Now

God is here, but we take His presence for granted. The fact of His presence is well understood, but people rarely understand the true significance of His presence. Think about the powerful implications of His presence. If you know that God is here, how could you sin, despair, or quit? Would you steal if the owner of the store were watching you?

It is said that no one is without sin. We can therefore conclude that when sin occurs it is because the sinner set God aside, or disappeared God from his thoughts. The fact is that He didn't go anywhere, but we shushed Him out of our reality—much like the myth that an ostrich will bury its own head in the ground to make its predator disappear. Or maybe we had a sinful lapse of the real, and merely forgot that God is eminent. To keep faith, remind yourself regularly of His presence— especially when temptation approaches.

He Has Told Me in His Word

God has made a promise and He'll keep it. We believe that He will resurrect the dead—why not believe His other promises, as well? It's odd that some people are sure of the resurrection, which would be nothing short of miraculous, but doubt that God will provide protection and sustenance, which people are able to provide for themselves. Why is it easier to believe in His miracles but not the mundane? Human nature likes to trust in a higher power, especially if there are no immediate ramifications of that trust. However, putting your faith in Him to feed and shelter you and your family could have immediate, disastrous results if it doesn't pan out. And so we take charge of these things for ourselves. There is no risk, but also no trust.

Helping others can endanger your life. We don't live in a Hollywood reality, where a makeover and a few hugs can transform a sinner into a saint. We do not get to write our own endings to life's story. Sometimes things go bad—real bad. You lose face, money, time, or worse. I accept suffering as a reality in faith. We know He is in control of outcomes and we are here for a moment. His way is perfect, unlike my understanding. We can trust Him, but will we? Remember, this is what we signed up for.

I propose that if you can't trust Him for the lesser things, you could not truly be trusting Him with your soul. Your soul and your body go hand in hand. If you believe He will bring about the resurrection, then you should be able to consistently trust Him to provide the lesser things. Therefore, determine to believe His Word. Read it and remind yourself of who He is and what He can accomplish through you.

He Showed Me

Many times, He calls us to a very specific job. Remember what He did to bring you to a certain place or situation. Do you remember how He brought you to where you are? The Word, divine appointments, dreams, and visions are all ways through which God can lead us. You see God use these methods throughout the Old and New Testament: Moses had a burning bush, Peter had a dream, and John had a vision.

God has moved me through these methods, as well. I once went to Afghanistan as the result of a dream. We started a radio program after much prayer and divine "coincidences." So keep your eyes open. Put dreams, visions, and other so-called coincidences together and sometimes you'll see the leading of God. I do not believe that every meeting or dream is the hand of God, but I stay open to the possibility.

I once dreamed that I was in a room full of missionaries in Afghanistan and I was in the center. In the dream I was weeping and the missionaries asked: "Why?" I wouldn't tell them. But I knew. I was supposed to take the director's role of that agency, and in the dream I didn't want to.

I realized that the dream may have been sent from God, so I took a step of faith. I contacted the agency and learned that they needed a director. My wife and I applied for the position, and the agency paid for our trip to Afghanistan. We met with the missionaries, like I had seen in the dream. I discussed with them the idea of me working there, and we had a heated discussion over the role and direction of the mission. I told them repeatedly that they wouldn't want me as director given our differences. They eventually agreed, and we returned home. I do not know what God was doing, but it was His leading hand and we simply trusted Him. It didn't go how I imagined, but it is His work.

When in distress do not question—just remember. Just like if you were rock climbing. After you set protection at a high point and begin to descend the cliff, you invariably start to wonder: "Did I do a good enough job putting in my protection?" Part-way down the wall, you may begin to question the safety of your rope and the protection. But, it is damaging to rethink it; it is too late. In this case, you must remind yourself that if you had not placed the protection well enough, you wouldn't have descended in the first place. In the same way, do not rethink the trip God sends you on; remember who He is and what He did to show you what to do.

He is in control, by the way. When I teach a person to climb, I show them that they can trust me and the protection. When they climb high enough to be concerned for their safety, I make them lean on their protective rope while I hold them in place. Then, I challenge them to come down. I tell them to let go of the rock and jump to me. But they can't.

No matter how they try to jump, they cannot because I have the other end of the rope. The rope strength, the protection holding the rope, and me holding the rope gives them security. They can't jump. Therefore, how could they fall?

They can't jump because I have control. This is how it is with God. When you are in His will, you can't fail. He is in control.

I said that He won't let you fail or fall. But God doesn't measure things the way we do. He will accomplish His purpose in you and me, but you may not find the success you thought might occur.

I Can See It

Look. When you daydream, you imagine both disasters and delights. It is important that you use your mind to work with your faith, not against it. We often imagine the potential negative outcomes of faith and obedience. We vividly visualize potential horrors. This imagination usually hinders our faith instead of bolstering it. Rarely do we use our minds to lift our faith! But why visualize disaster? Instead, you should focus on the end result: a God-centered and directed faith. Use the power of your mind to support your faith. See God as mighty and present and working for an outcome.

If you see only the potential for disaster and forget who God is, you're in trouble. If you only act when it is safe and you have control, can you say that you have faith?

If this is still how you operate, you must learn to walk in trust of Him. You do not need faith to do what you are able to do, but for what is beyond you. When the opportunity comes to trust Him and obey, many people will invent a way to solve the issue that keeps themselves safe. This is sin!

See in your mind what He will do and make this vision match your prayers. Obey Him in trust. Push out negative, anti-faith thoughts and see what is consistent with your faith, with the Word, and with wisdom.

I Don't Care What It Costs

Do not obey Jesus only if it feels good to do so. Faithful obedience is costly. Jesus on the cross is the only example we need to convince us of the cost of faith-obedience. Become someone who says "yes," no matter what the cost. We say "yes" because Jesus did. We do not quit because He did not.

This is Christianity, not Kiwanis. Nominal Christians can choose to obey or not. But blood bought lovers of God—just do it.

Never look at the possible negative outcomes as determinants of obedience. When you have been shown what to do, the potential costs do not matter. Remember that Israel wandered in the desert for forty years after disobeying God's call to enter the Promised Land. They had many good reasons to fear his command. They wondered that they would not be successful, that many would die, that their families would be torn apart. But in the end, they regretted their decision to disregard God's will.

Right now, I want to help you remove the excuses you make to wriggle out of the Savior's embrace. We ought to count the cost, pray, do the wise planning, and then…? Take action.

He Will Not Forsake Me

God is good. He won't quit on us. He will not lead us and then drop us. When you're under stress and the pressure builds—when the world is stacked against you—remember. His son felt abandoned on the cross, but remember the victory! God makes miracles happen when times are hard—not when you are protecting yourself with a self-imposed, cultural prison of self-reliance! You do not need faith for little things—the devil's spawn survive without faith every day.

You may at times feel abandoned, but that is an illusion—a demonic attempt to blind you. God says he will never leave or forsake us. It may be difficult to keep your faith, but He will keep His promise. This trust you have in Jesus will plow through obstacles like a bulldozer. You need it for the impossible. You will become the very will of God, smashing these three dimensions and time, overcoming the natural to do his will. Remind yourself not to quit. When you know that He loves you, that He is going to use you, and that nothing can stop Him, you will walk in the real-real with the Messiah.

Do Not Look Back

The Bible says, "Let us not become weary of doing good."[5] When you look at the loss, the pain, and the distress you may be suffering, you can lose sight of the facts of what faith allows you to see. Then, it is all too easy to just quit.

Do not look back. You'll become mesmerized by the fantasy of past losses. But this sense of loss is illusory. There is no real option. You cannot quit. Even if you long for the past, there is no way back. You will have

---

[5] Gal 6:9

burned the bridges for retreat. As Jesus says, "No one who puts his hand to the plow and looks back is fit for service in the kingdom of God."[6] Finishers win and losers quit!

Be Decisive

When God's Word and His leading direct you, you must follow. Do it now! You need to dwell on action and duty and not on the potential for worldly loss. I have all the same tendencies as you, after all. I love my kids, my life, and family. I want to take it easy, too. But I was able to overcome this fear and follow where God led. And you can, too. We must not give in to the temptation of an easy life.

I have challenged myself for years to do the hard thing. Once, some friends and I were jumping into a pool located below a balcony. I was scared. I tried to convince myself to jump, but I was frozen. Then a little girl stood on the rail next to me and jumped without hesitation.

That was it! I decided to change.

Since then, I've had opportunities to do the same. Once my kids were jumping off a very high bridge into a lake. I decided that I would do it, too. I took off my shoes,

---

[6] Luke 9:62

threw off my shirt, walked to the rail, climbed up, and jumped. It was wonderful not to be burdened by that fear any longer.

Similarly, those who wish to follow the path of God must not be controlled by fantasies of doom. These limit us. They keep us from doing good to all. We become locked in fear and create reasons for why we can't act. This fear is horrible bondage for those who believe we can do all things through Christ, who strengthens us. When opportunities arise to do good, just jump!

Please give up; surrender to Him. Take up your cross, deny yourself, and follow Jesus.

RESOLVE

Do you only help if it's easy? What if you suffer alongside those you would help? Pain and suffering are a test of your faith. Without determination, it is too easy to quit loving as you are commanded.

First, you must accept that it is normal to suffer for doing the right and loving thing. Look at Luke 6:22–23:

> Blessed are you when men hate you, when they exclude you and insult you and reject your name as evil, because of the Son of Man. Rejoice in that day and leap for joy, because great is your reward in heaven. For that is how their fathers treated the prophets.

And also look at Matt 5:11-16:

> Blessed are you when people insult you, persecute you and falsely say all kinds of evil against you because of me. Rejoice and be glad, because great is your reward in heaven, for in the same way they persecuted the prophets who were before you. You are the salt of the earth. But if the salt loses its saltiness, how can it be made

> salty again? It is no longer good for
> anything, except to be thrown out and
> trampled by men. You are the light of the
> world. A city on a hill cannot be hidden.
> Neither do people light a lamp and put it
> under a bowl. Instead they put it on its
> stand, and it gives light to everyone in the
> house. In the same way, let your light shine
> before men, that they may see your good
> deeds and praise your Father in heaven.

It is blessed to suffer for righteousness sake. Jesus says that this is true. Embrace these scriptures, they help give firmness to our understanding of the will of God.

What does Jesus say about avoiding such suffering? In Luke 6:26, He says, "Woe to you when all men speak well of you, for that is how their fathers treated the false prophets."

Abel, Noah, Moses, the prophets, John the Baptist, Jesus, the disciples, Paul, and the historic martyrs even until now have suffered, validating these truths. Follow their example of love and faith.

Historic Perspective

Many Biblical characters have stuck it out during tough times. So did Richard Wurmbrand of Romania under

Russian communists and Corrie ten Boom under the Nazis in Holland.

The prophet Daniel prayed after the King's edict, even though he knew the potential consequences of his opposition. So it says in Daniel 6:10–12:

> Now when Daniel learned that the decree had been published, he went home to his upstairs room where the windows opened toward Jerusalem. Three times a day he got down on his knees and prayed, giving thanks to his God, just as he had done before. Then these men went as a group and found Daniel praying and asking God for help. So they went to the king and spoke to him about his royal decree: "Did you not publish a decree that during the next thirty days anyone who prays to any god or man except to you, O king, would be thrown into the lions' den?"

Another example is in Daniel 3:16–23, when three Jewish people refused to bow to the King in worship and were to be punished.

> Shadrach, Meshach and Abednego replied to the king: "O Nebuchadnezzar, we do not need to defend ourselves before you in this matter. If we are thrown into the blazing

furnace, the God we serve is able to save us from it, and he will rescue us from your hand, O king. But even if he does not, we want you to know, O king, that we will not serve your gods or worship the image of gold you have set up."

Then Nebuchadnezzar was furious with Shadrach, Meshach and Abednego, and his attitude toward them changed. He ordered the furnace heated seven times hotter than usual and commanded some of the strongest soldiers in his army to tie up Shadrach, Meshach and Abednego and throw them into the blazing furnace. So these men, wearing their robes, trousers, turbans and other clothes, were bound and thrown into the blazing furnace. The king's command was so urgent and the furnace so hot that the flames of the fire killed the soldiers who took up Shadrach, Meshach and Abednego, and these three men, firmly tied, fell into the blazing furnace.

When in pain or surround by fear, our desire to continue to do good weakens and it is hard to carry on. When we begin a project, we often look forward with optimism that overshadows the negative. Our optimism swarms our fear and doubt.

But, when under pressure we tend to lose optimism and compromise on our goals. Any way to escape from the pressure will suffice in that moment!

When I wrestled, I trained hard. At times, I wanted to quit. Our coaches were constantly pushing us to improve our physical fitness. As a freshman I felt like I was dying partway through the first practice. I looked at the coach from under my physical strain and asked, "How much longer?" He replied, "Thirty-five minutes." We had only been going for ten minutes! I thought I couldn't go on, but felt that I had to. The thought of thirty-five more minutes made me want to cry.

Over the stretch of four years as a wrestler, I learned to persevere while in pain. I had to build an "I do not quit" attitude. I learned to persist, no matter what the cost. Finishers win and losers quit!

Wurmbrand told the story of a man in a Romanian prison who was required to run for seventeen hours a day. He did this without a break for over twenty years. When asked how he did it, the man replied, "Singing! Singing!" He learned to persevere using sincere praise.

We can bear the costs of obedience with the strength of our faith and sincere praise. Practice this now, before your burden makes you doubt your course.

Call to Carry On

We are called to carry on. This is how the world knows we are His. Without this pressure, the world would have difficulty distinguishing the saints from those people who merely avoid wrongdoing rather than actively pursuing the right. This is the light and salt—not merely that we are better workers or more loving fathers than most, but that we are called by God and carry on in His name.

The Bible requires us to persevere. In the future, under the pressure of this new age, the Church will be tested. This will determine who are truly His.

Thus, according to Heb 10:36–39:

> You need to persevere so that when you have done the will of God, you will receive what he has promised. For in just a very little while, "He who is coming will come and will not delay. But my righteous one will live by faith. And if he shrinks back, I will not be pleased with him." But we are not of those who shrink back and are destroyed, but of those who believe and are saved.

Can you see how important perseverance is to our security? Faith and perseverance are tied together. We believe that He saves those who are faithful to Him and that salvation is a reward; consequently, we endure.

Revelations 13:7–10 also reveals how God desires patient endurance and faithfulness:

> [The Beast] was given power to make war against the saints and to conquer them. And he was given authority over every tribe, people, language and nation. All inhabitants of the earth will worship the beast—all whose names have not been written in the book of life belonging to the Lamb that was slain from the creation of the world. "He who has an ear, let him hear. If anyone is to go into captivity, into captivity he will go. If anyone is to be killed with the sword, with the sword he will be killed." This calls for patient endurance and faithfulness on the part of the saints.

How to Hang in There

Endurance in doing good is an essential issue. Not endurance in meeting the standards of cultural morality, but endurance in maintaining Christ-like righteousness. Cultural morality is about caring for the globe, caring for the community through walk-a-thons for breast cancer, mowing your lawn, attending Little League baseball games and Mother's Day brunches. But being like Jesus is a larger sacrifice you make in order to care for the needs of the world according to the will of the Father. Living a Christ-like life is superior to following cultural morality, which is always shifting and characterized by pharisaical showmanship.

I want to remind you of the four components of endurance: the Body of Christ, the Spirit of Christ, the Words of Christ, and the Service of Christ. These components must be balanced. Each is essential for longevity.

The Body is made of His people. Not any person will do. They must be active in the pursuit of obedient living and faith, meet with these people regularly outside of the Sunday service, tell stories of encouragement and action, and encourage the other components. We need their involvement. They lift us up and inspire, giving us courage and strength. This band of brothers suffer with us through our trials and work at our side.

The Spirit guides and councils us. Through Him, we see and know. He shows us where to go and what to do through prayer and meditation, in accordance with the Word. The Holy Spirit dwells in the follower and guides us. As stated in Rom 8:14, "...those who are led by the Spirit of God are sons of God."

We know truth by His Word. We live by the knowledge of His Word, which protects us from confusion and doubt. He tells us how to live, what to think, and even how to think. He keeps us positive under pressure. It brings light to our circumstances and actions. Through the Bible, we see His heart and attitude, what He rewards and punishes.

In His service, we are given healing and soundness of mind. Since we focus on helping others in their distress, our minds aren't concerned about ourselves. This is such a freedom. Imagine not thinking about yourself. What a liberty! This freedom makes you light and capable of overcoming your challenges, as well as those of others. When I'm busy with service, I feel refreshed working alongside Jesus. What a safe, secure place this is.

This is how we endure securely. With the components of endurance, we can persist greatly. His Body, Spirit, Word, and Service are elemental to kicking down the work of the Devil and rescuing those he has enslaved. And it will protect your soul from the enemy's inevitable attacks.

Thus far, you have uploaded quite a bit of philosophy on compassionate living. Philosophy is valuable if it can manifest as a workable plan. Thus, it is time to develop a plan for compassionate living, for a life that will help to solve the social problems we are faced with today.

You've discovered the cost of service and the persecution that inevitably comes. We've discussed the necessity of faith and the resolve necessary to finish the job. The next step will teach you a few essential components and how to properly use them in the endeavor to follow God's plan for you.

To accomplish this great task of transformation, we need to use prayer and Bible reading. Prayer is used purposefully and the Bible is used as a reference to lead us over the rough terrain of service. You also need a community and a network to support you. You cannot do anything alone; your friends, family, and acquaintances provide necessary reinforcement for your effort.

Prayer

Our understanding of prayer needs to change. Most Christians talk about spiritual warfare but don't really know what it is, what it is really about, and why it is important that we fight. This is due to the fact that most Christians have had limited engagement in our purpose. Prayer is not simply something that we ought to do. It is not merely something that gives us hope when we are low—it is more than the obligation we feel if we want a blessing. We often neglect prayer and feel a little guilty about this neglect, which I find odd in those who say we aren't under law any longer.

Prayer is a right and protection. It is given to those who have submitted to God provided to the children of God because of Jesus' sacrifice. Prayer keeps us tuned to truth and provides hope when the situation seems difficult or improbable.

This defense is necessary for the sake of your soul. Demonic forces are at work to destroy your faith. Remember, without faith we can't please God; devoid of faith, we will not obey. How can you gain salvation if you won't trust Jesus? You cannot be saved without faith. Your soul is at stake.

Read the Lord's Prayer, which we are called to pray, Matt 6:9–13:

> This, then, is how you should pray: "Our Father in heaven, hallowed be your name, your kingdom come, your will be done on earth as it is in heaven. Give us today our

daily bread. Forgive us our debts, as we also
have forgiven our debtors. And lead us not
into temptation, but deliver us from the evil
one."

This is your protection. "And lead us not into temptation, but deliver us from the evil one." Why pray this if we do not need God's help to overcome temptation? Of course we need it. Paul said that the enemy is scheming and planning against us, that he is like a roaring lion looking to devour us.

I pray the Lord's Prayer in my own vernacular:

Lord, I desire that I would worship you as
you deserve and the world would see you
as you are and revere you. I ask that you
would perform a changing work in leaders
and individuals of this world so that we
would live as you would have us and to love
as you have taught us, unafraid.

Please provide for me, my family, and my
friends: we can do nothing without you.
Forgive me my inconsiderate sins, which are
ultimately against you. I will forgive all
debts and hurts that others have
thoughtlessly committed against me. I know
I have no power against the enemy except
what you have given. Please protect me,

that I may love fearlessly with a whole
heart.

As members of today's society, we face many obstacles to faith. We experience personal disappointments and betrayals at every turn. When we give our time, money, and care faithfully in the pursuit of God's will, we can be disappointed that those whom we serve often do not change and sometimes revile us. You and I need Him to support us and encourage us to keep going. Pain and disappointment are destined to come. We will need Him to remind us of Christ's suffering on the cross and that this sacrificial life is how we will live and die. Let us resign ourselves to His way of salvation for the world.

This war for our souls and the world's is well depicted in the scriptures. Ephesians 6 shows us that the fight is normal and must be fought. We know that the devil is scheming against us, bringing evil upon us, and that the many seemingly natural misfortunes that fall upon us are truly from the enemy.

The Church of God must live by trusting Him. We are required to do what He shows us is right and not give in to fear. We must be alert and ready. His truth must be ours; we must rigorously yield to it. His words are our guide. He will give the prize that belongs to His faithful. We must stand strong and pray in His will for ourselves and others who are servants in war.

The Bible

In order to truly follow God's will, we must use the Bible differently than we have before. Our situation is more challenging now that we are serving powerfully. We are caring for people in complex situations, and it costs us much more to do so than to care only for ourselves. The Bible provides us with instruction on how to deal with the difficult issues we will face.

Many who are reading this might feel as though they know the scriptures pretty well. I suspect that you have read the Bible through multiple times, heard many sermons, and read a few good books. In spite of this knowledge, most people have some Biblical blind spots, even when it comes to many well-known verses.

Take the following scripture quiz to see how well you know the Bible.

1. Galatians 6:7–10:

> Do not be deceived: God cannot be mocked. A man reaps what he sows. The one who sows to please his sinful nature, from that nature will reap destruction; the one who sows to please the Spirit, from the Spirit will reap eternal life. Let us not become weary in doing good, for at the proper time we will reap a harvest if we do

not give up. Therefore, as we have opportunity, let us do good to all people, especially to those who belong to the family of believers.

Answer the following question: What is the harvest you will reap?

2. John 15:1–17:

I am the true vine, and my Father is the gardener. He cuts off every branch in me that bears no fruit, while every branch that does bear fruit he prunes so that it will be even more fruitful. You are already clean because of the word I have spoken to you. Remain in me, and I will remain in you. No branch can bear fruit by itself; it must remain in the vine. Neither can you bear fruit unless you remain in me.

I am the vine; you are the branches. If a man remains in me and I in him, he will bear much fruit; apart from me you can do nothing. If anyone does not remain in me, he is like a branch that is thrown away and withers; such branches are picked up, thrown into the fire and burned. If you remain in me and my words remain in you, ask whatever you wish, and it will be given you. This is to my Father's glory, that you bear much fruit, showing yourselves to be my disciples.

As the Father has loved me, so have I loved you. Now remain in my love. If you obey my commands, you will remain in my love, just as I have obeyed my Father's commands and remain in his love. I have told you this so that my joy may be in you and that your joy may be complete. My command is this: Love each other as I have loved you. Greater love has no one than this, that he lay down his life for his friends. You are my friends if you do what I command. I no longer call you servants, because a servant does not know his master's business. Instead, I have called you friends, for everything that I learned from my Father I have made known to you. You did not choose me, but I chose you and appointed you to go and bear fruit—fruit that will last. Then the Father will give you whatever you ask in my name. This is my command: Love each other.

Answer the following question: How do you remain in Christ?

I venture to say that most if not all will give the wrong answer. Not because you are stupid or illiterate, but because you received a different philosophy than Christ's in the Church—perhaps the right information, but with the wrong emphasis. Truly, I think I could ask many pastors and they might get the wrong answers for the same reasons.

Recently, I listened to a well-known pastor on Youtube. He spoke on remaining in Jesus. He blew it! He got it wrong, because he has been influenced by the larger Christian community for years. If this were a trivial issue, it would be no big deal, but these two scriptures expose a critical misunderstanding of what is at stake in the faith and how we are to live. Our proper understanding of the scripture will affect our behavior.

The answers are not hidden, they are written in the text. You do not require special training or seminary to understand it.

Question 1 answer: In Galatians, the harvest mentioned is eternal life, not the salvation of souls, which is the common answer.

Question 2 answer: To remain or abide in Christ is to live in sacrificial love. In John 15, Jesus states that in order to remain is his love or abide, in order to remain one must to obey, and in order to obey one must love. Finally, he describes the type of love: a life laid down for others. The common answer is prayer, meditation, walking in the Spirit, or memorizing scripture. John 15 mentions none of these.

How did you do? What this exercise shows is that we might be reading the Bible not for what it actually says but for what we think it says. We pour our ideas into the scriptures, overlaying assumptions made from the philosophy derived from our culture, our Biblical teaching, and our misunderstanding of the Gospel.

We must read the scripture for motivation, in order to understand our responsibility, in order to see how Jesus lived, and in order to know how to work with people. The Acts church cared for the needs around them: Jesus came to preach the Gospel to the poor and Paul was called to remember the poor, which he said he was eager to do. The scriptures are abundant in wisdom you can use to solve difficult problems. But your reading must be founded on the correct understanding of the scripture and its application. Your reading must be founded on the cross, on love.

Here lies the problem. What is love and what does the cross teach us? Love is more than simple fondness for someone or empathy over someone's pain and problems. I recently read a Facebook posting that showed a picture of a Seattle homeless man; the response to this picture is one that is almost universal among "good" Christians:

> Lord, we ask You to protect those who have no home. Lord we ask for your help. Warm them when it's cold, cool them in warm weather. Let miracles happen, Lord. See their plea for help. Nobody should have to live his life on the streets, constantly looking for something to eat. Father in Your name I pray. Help them. Amen.

But this simple prayer does not fulfill Jesus' command to love. All too often, it is in our power to alleviate problems, but instead we pray. Prayer is a cheap way out—it costs us nothing. Prayer is good but blasphemous when you won't act. That is why James 2:16–17 states, "If one of you says to him, 'Go, I wish you well; keep warm and well fed,' but does nothing about his physical needs, what good is it? In the same way, faith by itself, if it is not accompanied by action, is dead."

Do you see? We feel very comfortable saying "No" to those around us who need our help, thinking that we are justified because we have an excuse.

Jesus has called us to help the less fortunate. That is why we are full of the Holy Spirit and his power—the power to love. But, as Ghandi wrote so disparagingly: "I like your Christ, I do not like your Christians. Your Christians are so unlike your Christ."

The cross shows us how He is and what He wants us to be like. That is why it is the defining element of the Christian that Jesus dies for sinners. But he asks us to do the same in turn. It is your turn now to "die," in that you give your life for sinners. Think of all the scriptures exhorting that we "die to self," and all the scriptures that reflect this principle.

Such as 2 Cor 5:14–15, which states:

> For Christ's love compels us, because we are convinced that one died for all, and therefore all died. And he died for all, that those who live should no longer live for themselves but for him who died for them and was raised again.

This idea of self-sacrifice is what identifies us and rages in the face of the anti-Christ. It is anti-Christ to do other than what He would do. We suffer with Christ for the salvation of many, for mercy, and for compassion. This is what he asks us to do: to become as God, to lead a Christ-like life.

Community

We should use community to support us in a life of service. In a normal Protestant congregation, from

Pentecostal to Lutheran, all communities are virtually the same. It can be broken into four types of people: pastors and other leaders, the faithful few, the regular attendees, and the inconsistent or first-time visitors. Some of these gather outside of church service for meetings, at small groups, Bible studies, and social events. You can take or leave these activities. They are not obligatory and rarely are they more than social or informational.

The church meeting starts generally with prayer, followed by worship music. Then come announcements and the sermon, which is usually quite broad with a few enlightening tidbits from the scripture or of political or social interest. It is all true and Biblical and non-specific enough that it doesn't move us. Moreover, it does not challenge us to do anything more than what we already wanted: better relationships, a better family, a happy life, and the salvation of our souls.

The congregation firmly "believes" in Jesus and His Gospel and all members are certain they will spend eternity with God because of the strength of their "belief." When you look at it this way, it is easy to see why so many Christians rarely attend church, if at all. Why go? They are already Heaven-bound; their work is done. They think that good works are not obligatory, but just pleasant afterthoughts that put jewels in their crowns. I don't know about you, but I do not need jewels; it would be much more fun to skip church on Sundays, if I could get to heaven without it. This is the conclusion drawn by many.

Community is to be formed around a mission, much as a baseball team works for the common goal of a win. For the sake of a common cause, people from different backgrounds unite to play by the rules, work together, and win. In this, camaraderie is formed through a common fight. You need a community that supports your action. This community must understand and advocate the mandate. It must actively support and encourage the work. This Church must organize and form a plan to act.

I'm not suggesting that your church isn't good enough. You have to work with what you are given. I'm merely giving a picture of how it should be done. The Church must state the clear mandate and continually enlighten the congregation on the practical side of sacrificial living. It must encourage action that supports that mission.

My congregation is formed around a mission. Of a normal church, it is commonly said that 20% of the people do 80% of the work. In ours, 80% of the people do about 95% of the work. This is so for two reasons: because the mission is clear and because the mission is encouraged. Those not interested in Christian service slip off to a church with less demanding "gospel." I encourage them to stay and join in this community of service, but if they leave for cheap grace I'm happy to see them go.

Network

I recognize the difficulty of all that I am revealing. With a job and family, how can you significantly improve anyone else's life when you have only so much money and time? But it is not an option to do nothing. We will have to drastically modify how we live to change the focus of our life because we are called. It is our responsibility to help others because of the love mercifully given us. So we have a dilemma!

The network is the answer.

Your network will involve people and social groups, including your closest friends and family. Together, you will form your own network.

You can also use a group that already exists. You and your small team can volunteer at homeless feeds or clothing give-a-ways to the poor. There are thrift stores specifically developed for outreach to those who might need your help. People who have outreach systems already in place are great to team with, especially when you are just getting started.

My network has developed a website at http://www.operationdeuge.com that provides encouragement and resources. Operation Deluge is designed to support you in your efforts to help others in need and to solve the problems associated with this effort. The site will link you with people all over the country who are determined to carry out Christ's mandate.

This will begin to provide, at minimum, an addendum to the community you need. The camaraderie in the common cause will help sustain you in this work. It isn't a substitute for Church, but an incredible enhancement.

With the people you gather, the social groups you volunteer with, and Operation Deluge, you will have the additional support you need to help people.

These work together to give vision, encouragement, correction, and challenge. This will make it possible to do what you may never have expected. The work He'll perform through you and your friends is amazing and powerful.

Volunteering

You volunteer to provide an opportunity to meet and serve those who are outcast. Certainly, you are there to support the goals of the organization at which you serve. You are there to enhance the organization by doing what other volunteers might find to be a little over the top: caring for them individually and personally.

Yesterday, I was assisting at a feeding program. I help with food preparation and hospitality. I smile and greet people and mind my own business. I did not want to impose myself, but just be a friendly, helpful ornament of the program. Then I saw a person who had lived with me for a few months some years ago. We rekindled our friendship and I got to practice my Spanish on him. He lives in his car and goes to a Hispanic church.

I asked him how he was doing and he told me of his problems. He had lost his girlfriend and was without work. I offered him a place to stay, but he was happy with the independence that his cool, damp import provided. He was full of excitement to serve God, with his Spanish tracts and Study Bible. To encourage his work of evangelism, I gave him the money in my pocket.

Today, I saw him again. He wanted to buy a TV with a built-in DVD player, assuring me that it was not for secular entertainment but to fill the boredom of his lonely car. He would use it to watch Christian videos. I didn't give him any money for it, however. I didn't give him money because it wasn't a need, and I knew that he saw me as an easy target.

We volunteer to interact with the people of need. We get to know them and invite them to move forward in their lives. We discover their needs and find how we can assist.

Conclusion

It is important to recognize that a lifestyle of service requires stamina. Jesus intends for us to be exhibited on the cross like him; according to 2Cor 5:15: "…no longer live for themselves but for Him."

With a developed community of support for this Christian life and a network to provide assistance to the broken, you can have a huge effect on the world around you. Jesus will see your devotion and be pleased.

PROBLEM ANALYSIS PROCESS

Like a doctor, you must perform a thorough diagnosis of the individual you would help. A good doctor compares how the body should function with how it is currently functioning. He then provides a plan for helping his patient attain normalcy. Like a doctor, you must understand the person and the barriers that hinder him or her from approaching normalcy. Normalcy in this case is the ability to hold a job, to have a family, and to maintain good relationships in the community.

A doctor's examination must be rigorous. The doctor must understand the body and how it works. Without these two essential ingredients, the doctor cannot design an accurate treatment plan. It is vital that we care for souls in the same way that a doctor cares for bodies. Thus, we must be armed with thorough diagnostic tools and a wealth of knowledge.

Analysis

We must be skilled at analyzing our friends' difficulties. As I have previously written, the problems of each individual are caused by the unique conglomeration of facts surrounding him or her. You must spend time considering the person's immediate situation and how it connects to the past. You must understand his or her skills and attributes while recognizing the issues that bar the person from maintaining normalcy.

I recently brought home a romantically involved pair of transients. They aren't married and have recently met. They are from Texas and currently live in a tent north of Seattle. They have no money, no professional skills, and no education. They are both in their early twenties. Jim recently left Texas because of a death threat. His mother and brothers were recently killed; his uncle killed one of the killers and is currently in prison. Jim's girlfriend has learning difficulties and is confused, maybe from drugs or experiences from her past. Neither one has formal identification.

First we gave them a place to live and took them out of the cold rain. We gave them food and a shower, and let them wash their clothes. Sheila had an infected leg, and so we made sure that she got care. During this time, we got to know the couple. They couldn't get jobs without IDs, so we began the process of retrieving their birth certificates from Texas.

The analysis comes through interaction. Bit by bit, the picture of their life comes together through daily interaction. How can you tell if they are lazy? The answer comes when you see that they won't help the family or look for a job. How do you know if they are afraid of making a change? You will learn by knowing their story and observing their actions and reactions. Do they have training, a GED, a felony? You will find out over time and will be able to help them overcome whatever obstacles stand in their way.

Some refuse to move forward. When I'm confident that this is the case, I kick them to the curb with an invitation. They leave knowing that when they are ready to take charge of their future, I am available to help.

Some people will just need permanent help. Some are so mentally and emotionally damaged they cannot work formally. So we give them the opportunity to help around the house, with yard work and dishes, for example. This way they know they can always find work when they feel that they are able. Unfortunately, because of the Social Security checks that most receive, they have little incentive to stay and normalize to their potential. They generally move on and are sort of oblivious to anything but the immediate. They turn into vagabonds once more.

Think about how to help people in need in ways that will benefit them in the long term. Some people just give money to homeless people, but how will that really help beyond the needs of the day? All that contributes to is a career as a beggar. I have heard of people giving homeless people a two-for-one coupon for McDonalds. The guy it was given to laughed, because he didn't have money for the one to get the free one. I even heard of a benevolent Christian giving the homeless food—a frozen turkey at Thanksgiving.

Normalcy

What is normal? Different people will tell you different things. However, for the context of this book, normalcy is about meeting certain standards of education, training, employment, living conditions, lack of substance abuse, and relationships that are necessary to survive and thrive in the current socio-economic system.

Living Conditions

If the people you are trying to help do not have a permanent, sanitary residence, find them a place to live with you or your friends. Your church will surely help in this endeavor. Once they have steady work, they should then begin setting money aside for housing. You can help this process by working with them to build a budget and by discussing the pros and cons of their various housing options.

Education

Education is a necessary prerequisite for most jobs. People in need may not have finished high school, and so one of the first steps to achieving normalcy is to help them get their GED. This will mean going to the community college and helping them sign up for the class, ensuring that they attend, and providing the help they need to pass the test.

Training

Anyone looking to enter the workforce needs skills in order to sell themselves for a position. Technical colleges and community colleges provide many skills-building classes, such as welding, mechanics, dental assistant, and other types of training. Depending on their goals, some people may want to get an advanced degree. Even earning a food handler's permit can be helpful.

Beyond college classes, some churches have congregants with small businesses that can provide on-the-job training.

Employment

When it comes to finding employment, a strong network can be a job hunter's greatest asset. This is particularly true of someone who has been homeless, as many employers might not hire such a person without a reference or someone to vouch for him or her. In order to help the needy find a job, give them your network. Ask friends, family, the church, and other acquaintances if they know of possible places where your newly trained and educated person can work. Most of the work we have found for those we've helped was found through our network.

Substance Abuse

Almost all those we will help will use drugs and alcohol. There are many favored remedies. I do not personally think it matters how one goes about being free from this destructive behavior. We are all aware of Alcoholics Anonymous, Narcotics Anonymous, Christian 12 Step Programs, and Drug and alcohol counseling. Each individual will have their preferences.

I prefer none of the above, although I'm not critical of them. I simply have a note to add when using these methods. They are bridges not destinations. All these paths need to ultimately lead to Jesus. He is the reason for change ultimately.

Through Him we have a reason to change. The sin of substance abuse is simply another expression of a violation of God's design. It shouldn't be elevated to some supernatural kind of temptation. It is a sin as any other. Jesus says to repent from sin. In this is salvation. No repentance, no salvation.

Some argue that you can't know about the power of addiction unless you have experienced it. That makes sense to me. But I'm a human experiencing life also. I have temptation and pain and have found methods to overcome. I admit it could be different but the remedies are similar to all sin.

Others argue if one was able to kick-it they really were not addicted. How can they say that with any certainty? Anyway this is how the justification goes. But these assessments leave a person believing there is no hope for them. They believe they are overcome by a power formidable. They conclude God understands their addiction and makes concession. He will let them in Heaven in spite of his sin. This leaves us to believe that those of us who have no addiction have to repent but those "special" people get to Heaven another way. This is a damning opinion unsupported in scripture centered on a grave misunderstanding of the Bible and Human nature. They also inadvertently block real redemption through giving the addiction more power over the individual than God has power to deliver them.

Here is an indisputable argument against the supernatural power addiction has over people. They simply lack impetus. This is the proof. Put a gun to an addicts head. Tell him you'll blow his brains out if he uses the drug of his choice. If he is not suicidal, he will find in himself the ability to say no to save his own life. This is indisputable. If the power were as great as they say he would take the drug in spite of the immediate promise of death. So why does this work? What do we learn? The "victim" doesn't want to suffer immediate consequences for his actions. Therefore all he needs to quit is a big reason. In this case the gun and the prospect of death is enough.

No big reason to stop and no freedom. Some people stop for small reasons like their family or to save their own life. But ultimately one needs a bigger reason. God has given us the ultimate reason. If one doesn't quit they will have punishment in Hell. This is the gun to their head.

There are plenty of things that need to be done to support someone in recovery. But I'm not writing a book on how to help someone in recovery. I will provide support tools at operationdeluge.com that will assist you in this process.

Relationships

People who are doing well have good relationships. They have friends who are there to help and be helped. They feel supported and loved. The family relationships that you rely on might not exist for the individual you choose to help, so you will be an integral part of his or her growing network of friends.

In order for people to have a normal life, all of these elements must be in place. Most homeless people do not meet the requirements of any of these categories. You will have to prioritize and help them get busy to improve their lives.

Most are uneducated or unemployed because of very real problems that must be overcome. Some have a tough time learning, while others might have emotional and psychological barriers that prevent them from meeting employers' requirements. Thus, most needy people will need a more thorough diagnostic to move them forward from their current situation.

Diagnosis and Remedy

I guess it is self explanatory. Wherever you see that someone has an issue that prevents him from reaching normalcy, you must work with him to find a long-term solution.

If a fellow can't get a job, we must help him to figure out why. Maybe he has no training, or he has a big mouth. It is our job to help him discover why he has been unemployed and what he can do to become employable. Simply compare the experience of the individual with what is necessary for him to reach normalcy and help him remedy the problem. There is always a solution.

Follow Up

The relationships we form with those we help require maintenance. They will need encouragement and advice throughout their transformation. Every situation requires new solutions.

I would like to say that when you help people and give them your wisdom, you will be successful if you are persistent. Success is also dependant on their willingness to change, which is a giant variable that is out of our control. Success does not always come quickly. Remember operationdeluge.com, where you can connect and receive support from others who have done what you are doing, who can provide the encouragement and resources you need. We can help you.

Conclusion

I think we value the souls we care for. Therefore, they inspire from us good ideas and encouragement. We will need to continue to encourage and support them as long as it takes and as long as they do not quit. The feeling you will get when someone turns his life around will be a reward in itself.

You might wonder why I do not talk about giving the Gospel to those you help. The reason I don't talk about giving the Gospel to those you help is because your actions speak louder than any lecture you could give. When you help and love an individual like no one ever has, they will see the power of Christ's message. We are always living as Jesus and speaking of Him and His ways. It just starts to rub off.

You should take those that you help with you to meetings at church and to gatherings with friends. You should give wisdom that you've gained from the Word and your experiences serving, just as you would to anyone. I'm not shy about drawing people to Christ, but I'm strategic in timing and approach. For example, one young fellow told me that he wanted to get baptized. This would be a noble and right act if he wanted to follow Jesus. But I had reservations as to whether he really wanted to follow Christ. I spent half an hour explaining the cost of following Jesus, virtually trying to talk him out of baptism. I told him that converting meant no more dope or chasing girls, but creating a new life of serving others like Jesus. Even after I clarified the cost of serving Jesus, he got baptized and we still serve together today. After eight years, we are still helping him normalize.

He has a wife and two kids. They recently took on the load of two more children. These children are from another family we are helping who are both heroin addicts. This couple was doing well for a short while but one is in jail on the way to prison and the other is out of state running from the police.

It is a long process. But we have a lot more to give and more skills than we may realize.

FRUIT

The fruit of this work will dramatically influence the world around you. It may surprise you to hear this—it may stretch your faith to believe that one person could change the world. I do not state this from mere hope; I believe what I read in the Word and I see the effect. This style of living has influenced my family by drawing them to a higher level of service. This lifestyle is gripping my friends through a series of uncomfortable nudges and pushing my church to be more involved. It is encouraging to note that many influential individuals of my community have been enlightened by the bold lifestyle I've been practicing.

Family

Since our children will create the society of the future, we need to provide them a lifestyle worth emulating. A living example is a powerful example. It can propel a person to goodness, although it can also plunge them into the Pit. We are living in a culture that in so many ways is luring our kids toward a devastating society. The church can do nothing to protect our youth, while the rest of the world just tells them to live and do what they like. Our culture offers pleasure at every turn, but we need to offer our children a purposeful life worth living.

Our culture is now exalting a socialistic agenda, based on the increased taxation of others in order to support the less fortunate. The up-side is its emphasis on helping others, even if the suggested mode is misguided. Bono of U2 is seductively offering an option that cares for the poor. He is helping make it popular to care for the poor. Protests of Wall Street are seemingly purposeful...and hip! In a world that seems filled with greed and injustice, it is all too easy for the youth of today to get caught up in goals of political upheaval. Someone should show that there is an alternative that can make a difference today without the passing of any law. Someone should show them that they don't need anyone's permission to start making a real change. Show them that we care more than the world does. We can do more in Christ's love with our own energy and resources than the U.S. government can.

My three oldest children are all in college. One is moving toward the life of purpose that I demonstrated to them, and the other two are dragging their feet. While they long to run to the world and enjoy it, they have been shown from childhood the truth of what we stand for. The guilt of not following this example stabs like shards of glass in the mind. It will not give them rest—their only release is submission to love.

My daughter is pursuing a career in education. Her developed skills and degree give her the opportunity to help her students beyond their basic education requirements, but to also help them improve all aspects of their lives. Her position gives her an opportunity to see the need early on in their lives, to help her students avoid a life like the ones experienced by those our family has helped. She is close enough to be aware of her students' real needs and influence them to lead a life of love and purpose.

Many of us have people in our lives who greatly influenced us. They were friendly and cared. Their encouragement gave us hope. I had a wrestling coach who was all I just mentioned. He was like a dad to me, but I think he was oblivious to the power he had to influence me. Such influence, when recognized, can be used to change lives in incredible ways.

My wife is similar to most other women in that she wants a secure and peaceful home, with a garden, where guests can visit on her time table. I do not think this is bad, and it is certainly not dreadful from a cultural standpoint. Unfortunately, it isn't Christian. Over time and with the help of the Word, my example, and coaching, my wife has changed her attitude from a tendency toward protectionism to a level of hospitality that is inclusive and open. If people drop in for dinner unannounced, they are fed and entertained as if they were an important invited guest. If I bring home someone who needs a place to stay, she happily produces a blanket and a soft place to sleep.

My daughter and her husband entertain new people often. Once they brought home two elderly men with mental health issues. One spoke to himself constantly and the other washed his hair in the sink multiple times a day. The hair-washer guy would pour coffee, dump some down the sink, and then add sugar and put the mug in the microwave. Without drinking any, he would do it all over again. Fifty times a day! Both of these men eventually left my daughter's home because they did not like rules. They also received Social Security checks. The street is freedom, paid for by the taxpayer.

The influence we exert in our family and the modification of life style that follows is profound and necessary to see "His Kingdom come and His will be done on Earth as it is in Heaven."

Friends

Our friends want to see Christ's life lived out; they deserve a living example of Jesus. We have tried to tell them about Jesus. They wonder if Jesus will change their life—they are afraid that they might change. When they think of Church people, they see friendly but quirky people. People who speak strangely, who never cuss and use Biblical language. We can't say "crap," but are authorized to say "pooh-pooh." We go to church and volunteer in Christian organizations that do not interrelate well if at all with the general public. They do not want to be like the Christians they see, who seem odd. But we can offer them something real, powerful, and convincing. If we live a loving and sacrificial lifestyle, they will see the change that a Christian can make in the world.

When you care for others as a way of life, you serve as a visible example of Christ's Word. You transform Christ's message from words about great people who lived two-thousand years ago into a clarion call for change today. As you care for a drug addict, you get several great opportunities to explain to others why you are reaching out to that person. You can tell them of the mercy you received and the obligation you now have to live mercifully. You can explain that there is no real difference between the person you're helping and you. Amazingly, you will not have a reasonable dispute about these ideas. If others differ with you, their reaction reflects the carnal reasons they will not extend mercy to others. They give the same reasons as many in the Church for not helping: it's dangerous and the people you help might take advantage of you. This is a natural response to the conviction and self justification that must come before repentance. Now, the self justification will come from either Christian or non-Christian. The power of this gospel is profound.

I have friends who are not Christians but admire us because of our lifestyle. In an age where people believe that the government should help the poor, these friends confess that it is even better to do it yourself. I have seen people who are not even Christians begin to help others in a deep, sacrificial way. In time, their sacrifice will lead them to recognize the source of the message. Jesus is the originator of this way. He is our leader, guide, and God.

I used to frequent a coffee house and use the internet. The owner, who was a middle-aged woman, became a friend of mine, and I told her our stories. She adamantly agreed with me that we, the church and community, should care for the poor. She was totally on board with a lifestyle of service.

Sometime later, she told me of a homeless woman she had met and wondered if I could help her. I squared off with her firmly but politely. I said, "And that is the problem. Everyone acts and speaks as though they care, but when push comes to shove they want a sucker who'll care in their stead."

She was shocked. We both knew what I was saying. I obviously would help the homeless woman, but I needed to take the opportunity to drive the nail deep in her mind.

One day I went back and she was so excited. "We brought her in and she is doing great!" she said with an exuberant smile.

This is the kind of influence we can have on our culture, if we insist.

Jesus gave stories and parables to explain the principles of love he was demonstrating in his life. In the same way, you can give people your stories of helping others. You can tell about how they are changing and how they hurt you, but that you continue loving. These stories are interesting, like a serial drama, and will maintain the attention of your audience. Best of all, they are laced with Jesus' love.

Your action and joyful suffering make so profoundly different and compelling a tale than the everyday events that most people experience. Your daring lifestyle stands in contrast to the security oriented, selfish, empty, and ultimately boring lives that people lead when their priority is security for themselves above all. In addition, those you tell about your lifestyle will have to reconsider whether they are living their lives the way they ought. It is hard for others to retain the lie that being a "good person" is enough when they see your righteousness demonstrated by your caring for others. It isn't about being braggadocios or "Look at me!" The emphasis is on showing others how God has shown us to live.

Do not get confused. This righteousness is Christ's being shown through you. These are His ideas, not mine. I would have never lived this way if He hadn't showed me how; it never crossed my mind to love strangers, to go out of my way to help people out of impossible situations. Jesus loves neighbors and enemies, the ungrateful, those who cannot repay, and even those who are unclean. How could I take credit, all Glory to God! I couldn't claim this righteousness as my own whatsoever—I lived so contrary to this love before I knew Him. He woke me up. He changed my mind and He demolished my previous idea of what it means to be a good person. My life just goes to show, "The Dude rocks—let me show you!"

Church

The church needs an option to the humdrum, empty, purposeless practices of religion that are commonly displayed in the modern gospel church. As you can sense, exposure to this lifestyle has an impact.

I interact with Christians from other churches often. I spend my time discussing these issues with examples. They are compelled by the message, but constrained by their wishful view of the Gospel of Love.

On one occasion, I spoke at a missions conference in Vancouver, Canada. The conference is attended by 20,000 people over the three-day event. I was to speak to 200 Christians.

Just before my talk on "What the Lost Love and Scares the Church," a young homeless guy asked me for money while I was outside drinking coffee at a Starbucks. I told him to sit down and have a coffee and visit. He said he was too busy and I responded, "You're not busy—you're homeless. You've got the time."

I bought him a latte and we talked. He told me of Matt 25: "When you have done this to the least of these you have done it unto me." These are the words of Christ that cast into Hell those who don't help the needy. I was shocked and told him I would give him $50 if he went with me to my seminar.

During the talk, I mentioned my new friend's needs. I told the attendees that he was a heroin addict and wanted help getting clean, and that he wanted a family to care for him. There were 200 of the best Christians in that room, but none raised their hand to help him. What a horrible witness! And yet, this is what we've come to perceive as normal.

My talk was bold and challenging after that. I'm sure I won't be invited back.

After the talk, a few brave women came and visited with me, shaken by what they had learned. Others scurried out. They were all impacted by the knowledge I had given them—that there was no middle ground left.

Community

Social services, courts, schools, and law enforcement can all be influenced through your giving lifestyle. These institutions have a perception of the world unchallenged by the people of the church. When we are involved in the lives of those involved with these workers it can change that perception and advance social awareness and advance necessary change in institutions.

I go to court with them and visit their lawyers, parole officers (PO's) and judges. Since interacting on this level I received calls for help from lawyers and PO's. After testifying in a Child Protective Services (CPS) case the judge stated "These people are doing it the way it should be done. They care for people on a personal level. The Social Services are like a broken cart with the wheels falling off."

My mother cared for the newborn infant of a young lady who had lost two children to CPS. She had become pregnant again, and the newborn was to be taken the same route as her older children, but my mother and sister-in-law intervened for the young lady with the social worker. They worked out a deal that allowed my mother to care for the baby while the young lady fulfilled the obligations to CPS that would allow her to get her baby back. The young woman lived with my brother and his family, and was able to spend lots of time with her baby.

Unfortunately, after about a year, the young lady quit and left her child. My mother is now adopting the little boy, even though she has great-grand kids already. What a time of life to start rearing a child! She loves the toddler, and so it doesn't seem a burden to her. He has brought her a lot of joy.

Conclusion

The church can perform as greatly as we expect it should. Something we have lacked in recent years is a dynamic witness. I recently read a poll that stated that 21% of non-churchgoers had no idea what positive role the church should play in the community, while only 27% knew that our job was to care for the lame, mentally ill, elderly, and all others in need. We need to change public perception. 80% should have been able unequivocally describe the church's true purpose. As you see, it is possible for us to meet this role. This is how we were meant to deeply impress upon the world who Jesus is and what He is like.

People are not generally resistant to love or Jesus. They are simply confused by us Christians. We proclaim love, but our compassion is different from theirs. We are controlled by the same fears as they are, and yet we say we have faith.

Why is it that the public can see the incongruence better than we can? Is it that we are blinded by fear and unbelief? Do we even really care? I choose to believe that we have been mislead by a partial message of the gospel: "Jesus loves you." And the pastor has left off the other part: "Go love them so they will know Me."

We have lacked those to lead us and show us the way. Those who lead us are produced in the laboratory of the seminary. The seminary emphasizes doctrine and intellect, so this is what they give us from the pulpit.

A lifestyle of service will make the broad impact of the Gospel felt. The public image of the church will be improved as a result, and the public will know that they need us. It will lift the general righteousness of the culture.

THE COST

The cost of serving Jesus is immense. It takes time, money, and entertainment. It requires you to alter your goals and dreams. It will use your family for a greater purpose than your amusement and fulfillment.

A typical life, even among Christians, is rooted in personal desires. After all, we consider "our" life to be ours! Which means we should be able to do with it what we please, right? Most people, therefore, use their lives for the purpose of serving themselves. Friends and family fit as resources for our needs, and we are willing to give to them and help them in order to maintain the life that we want for ourselves.

But our lives are not "ours"—they belong to God, who created us. We must not think of what we want, but of what He wants.

Jesus calls us to follow a different life than one of self-service. In Matt 5:46–47, he says, "If you love those who love you, what reward will you get? Are not even the tax collectors doing that?" There is no essential good in loving those who love us. That is easy—it comes without asking. Your love must extend past your family and friends, if you are to follow Jesus' way.

Time, Money, and Entertainment

"The pastor only wants my money!"

How many times have you heard this complaint? Well, it is partially true—but the culprit isn't the pastor. It is Jesus who wants your money. And not only that, He expects your time, as well. He is even so audacious as to require your life. As He says in Mark 8:35, "For whoever wants to save his life will lose it, but whoever loses his life for me and for the gospel will save it."

Who asks for so much? It is like we have offered Him a $100 bill, and he just smiles and asks for 99 more just like it. Shouldn't He be grateful for what we have already given?

But Jesus is worth everything you have. I know that you want to keep your life as your own. But you and I both know that we owe Him everything. Though you may say, "In my heart I gave him everything," it may not be true. What you do reflects your heart.

It's a head game that we play with ourselves, this sense that good intention is enough. But you cannot give Him only part of yourself and hold the rest back to serve only you. It is not enough to give a tithe and volunteer and call this our fulfillment of the call. This only amounts to an attempted bribe. But you cannot bribe the Incorruptible—He will not accept it.

You must live in His service. You must eat, exercise, and care for your children in order to fulfill God's purpose for this world. He will take care of us, but we have to give Him the same in return. He gave His Son, remember? Let God concern himself with us, and let us concern ourselves with Him.

Through the last few sentences, I feel like we have been wrestling in the dust. We must conquer our expectations, our plans for ourselves. With black eyes, sweat, and bloody lips, we shall proceed.

We work to provide for our families, and it is right that we do so.

But God also wants us to care for those about us who are in need. That is why Ephesians 4:28 reads: "He who has been stealing must steal no longer, but must work, doing something useful with his own hands, that he may have something to share with those in need."

You see, it is His intention that we provide for our family and supply for others. That is His plan.

Now, if we weren't professed supporters of Christ, we could simply take care of our own interests. With a self-satisfying gift to the poor, dropping a coin in the Salvation Army bucket, we could count ourselves as good people. It would fulfill our conscience to be sporadically benevolent.

Dancing while the house is burning is sensible for those who do not believe in tomorrow. As for we Christians, we know there is a tomorrow in Heaven and Hell. We know what our future will hold, but we must also live according to this knowledge.

Your life is not simply made for a forty-hour work-week, chores, and family. It is not meant for you to enjoy a few good times as you aim for retirement. That is not God's plan. Rather, your life exists for one goal: seeing that God's will on Earth will be as it is in Heaven.

First, you must align your reason for living with His purpose. Then, you must use the resources that God has given. In order to meet His will, you might change where and how you will live. You might reconsider the job you take and whether your spouse will work. You might buy a different car from the one you always wanted for yourself.

And you might find yourself forgoing "fun." By and large, our lives have been organized around our pleasure. Aligning your life to God's will might mean there are no more vacations, golfing, or movies in your future. But think not of "fun" as something that you deserve that you must give up—think of it as something you currently take at the expense of someone else's wellbeing. If everyone were more compassionate and less indulgent, there would be fewer hungry and homeless people. The decision to help others limits the money and time available for us to entertain ourselves. Truly, we replace the more shallow idea of fun with the satisfaction of honoring God through our service. While busy serving others' needs and fulfilling our obligation to God, we live as the poor, unable to enjoy the pleasures of what riches we may own, as did Jesus before us.

Family

The fact is that, as "poor" people, we have less in a worldly way. With less money and time, we have fewer choices. The kids might not be in Little League, or piano lessons might be too expensive. Private school is out of the question. Perhaps you can't afford a night out with your wife because you choose to serve Jesus. The risk that your family will resent the choice you have made is all-too-real.

Your family will be enhanced if you set the tone of Christ. Children value what their parent's value, and wives follow husbands who have a demonstrable conviction. Women admire men who are done with trivial pursuits.

I believe that service will help produce the best possible family and can produce a clear vision for compassionate living. I do not believe it will meet the Disney-family model requisites.

There is always the potential for collateral damage, as each person can respond differently to your exhibition of the lifestyle. But this lifestyle has an enormous positive effect on the family's view of the world. I believe this is good, but there is no guarantee that all members of the family will adopt the philosophy, as with any philosophy that you would apply to your family.

According to Barna research, the church is losing 80% of youth membership. Only 30 years ago, we were retaining 80%. Now, more than ever, we need parental modeling of the principle of sacrificial love. As we affected the youth of the past through the values of family, so we must in the present. Our religion has been presented without challenge or purpose at present. It has been me centered at best.

This model presents an inescapable picture. Through years of familial training, a normalcy of serving others can be imprinted on our children's minds. This training will be hard to escape. Inadvertently, the world reinforces this behavior through the latest tout for charity, generated from the Ghost of Christianity Past.

When a family has purpose, that purpose can galvanize the family unit. As the wife and husband unify over God's plan, the family stabilizes. The children are taught through experience the value of service and the plight of sin.

Please do not get the wrong idea. The Jesus lifestyle can be helpful and good for your family, but this is not a book that guarantees familial success through service. Two of my boys are running from this Christian responsibility, while my daughter is continuing the tradition of her childhood.

Above and beyond how family is benefited by service, your family is a tool that can help people, and also a way in which to build children who will grow to help people. With a family, it is easy to integrate into the greater community. Kids provide opportunities to interact in community activities. Single men roaming through parks may seem intimidating or dangerous, but a father and son are approachable. With a family, we can show broken homes how a family can function in love, as a whole. Family is an essential element in helping others. It is God's model.

Summation

Most people are driven by the goals and dreams that they create to fulfill their desires, whether they are high or low. But as Jesus states in Matthew 16:26, "What good will it be for a man if he gains the whole world, yet forfeits his soul? Or what can a man give in exchange for his soul?"

Christians must recognize that as God has given them life, so he demands it from them. We must therefore think what our Creator wants, rather than what we want. What are His goals and dreams?

We must submit our plans to Jesus. He will work in us and through us to do His thing. We have no other purpose except this. How can His will come on Earth as it is in Heaven, if not by the power of His Spirit through your life? Truly, He'll use you.

Does this seem too much to ask, that you yield your desires to fulfill His?

Remember, God is God and God is good. He gave His son to save us, and now we give our lives for Him as sons and daughters. We are His "Christ" on Earth, working His will in the present.

Jesus is in us, doing His thing if we allow Him.

PLAN

This chapter will give you a clear path and plan that you can use to help reach your potential. I think Christianity has been the only place that it is vogue not to plan. You've heard the idea that it's more spiritual to be moved by the Holy Spirit to action rather than to plan your action out ahead of time. This attitude is an easy trap. One of the gifts of the spirit is leadership, and planning is inherent to leadership.

The plan holds you accountable to your goals. If you wait to act until you feel like it or to when you get time, you may not act at all. You may never feel moved to act, and you'll instead use all your time on the things that immediately demand your attention. You'll never reach His expectations unless you plan the path that will lead you there.

The time to plan for action is always now.

Read

Here is a reading plan. It will help you to build your theological foundation, without which you will fall when trouble comes. We must develop the conviction that these scriptures are the Lord's call to Christians that urges us to serve the poor as He did. His call must be founded and reinforced in us if we are to follow through.

See operationdeluge.com for commentary on each section and view the podcast for each section.

Knowing God	Jeremiah 22:16
The True Fast	Isaiah 58
The Spirit of Christ	Matthew 5–7
New Attitude	Luke 6–7
Jesus, You and the Poor	Matthew 25:31–46
Lord's Prayer	Luke 11:2–13
Prig Debrief	

Pray

Take these scriptures to prayer. You'll need wisdom and strength, which He can provide. Solidify this foundation. With anticipation and hope, call on Him.

Talk

Tell others what you are learning. It will be interesting to them. It will not matter whether they are Christians or not. Their differences of opinion will lend toward great discussion; you'll be challenged and it will help harden your own convictions. As you speak, you clarify your understanding of Jesus' will. It will also help you to learn which friends you can rely on to support you in this endeavor, and will prepare your friends for the life-altering decisions you are about to make.

Invite

Make a list of friends, family, and other parties who might be interested in teaming with you. Then, invite them to coffee and desert in order to talk about what you are planning.

Use this outline for the meeting:

1. Welcome and thank you for coming.
2. Introduce those who do not know each other.
3. Pray for God's leading and wisdom for the extension of His Kingdom, in Jesus' name.
4. Show the introductory podcast from operationdeluge.com.
5. Refer them to this book and the Operation Deluge podcasts.
6. Discuss where you could volunteer.
7. Make plans to visit with an organization where you will offer support.
8. Plan for the next meeting.
9. Pray your thanks.

Group Plan

You need to decide together how you will work with and support one another. Where will you work? With whom will you work? How often will you meet to share stories and difficulties? How often will you undergo training and find encouragement from operationdeluge.com? Answering these questions will give you the structure you need to be substantially influential.

You are not alone. I am eager to coach and encourage you. I look forward to your blog posts on operationdeluge.com, which will be an encouragement to others. This is going to really keep us fired up.

Volunteer

Find a way to interact with the needs of others. Seek out a homeless outreach, food program, or clothing give-away. Some places to start your search include:

- The Salvation Army or similar groups.
- Social help groups that are publically funded.
- Where the poor go to get help.

Make a flyer and put it up in these places and invite people to get help from you.

Volunteer in a way that allows you to interact with the clients to discover their real needs. For example, if I could choose between volunteering as a cook or as a busser, I would pick busing. Bussing tables allows you to have more face-to-face contact with the people you would help.

You can also plan helpful training for these groups. Take a survey to discover their needs. While taking the survey, you will have an opportunity to have real discussions and get to know the people using the service.

Find the Need and Fulfill It

The object in volunteering is for you to find people with needs. A few days ago, I went to The Peer Connection, where mentally-ill individuals hang out. They play pool, use the internet, visit, and eat daily. I went and visited with a few of the staff. I sat with my lap-top across from a guy who had a lap-top computer also. I discovered that this guy had called me for help a few weeks before. He needed a travel-trailer moved from an impound lot. I gave him a business card, and he will call me when he is ready to move it.

Then the staff introduced me to a gal who was homeless. I gave her a business card with my name and number as well. Then another staff member brought me a young couple who were living in a tent. They only needed a blanket, but I went the extra mile and offered them a place to stay, where they would be protected from the horrible, rainy, winter weather of the Northwest.

Build Strength and Conviction

Meet with your group to pray and share your successes and concerns. Help each other and give each other suggestions; pray for one another.

Watch videos and read the biographies of those who have helped the poor. The biographies of William and Catherine Booth are excellent examples. And frequently check in with operationdeluge.com—it will be your spiritual battery charger, with regular updates and resources.

Help

You need to show your love for one another. Do not make any one person carry more than their share of the load. Help each other. Look at others and appreciate them. Notice what they do. Encourage the right spirit and attitude. Do not get jealous, gossip, or put each other down. Accept each person's individual gifts and use them.

Remember that you have your network because you cannot achieve God's will by yourself. You need each other, and this is why Jesus created a body to do His work, instead of just one man or woman.

There will always be a tendency to judge and back-bite. Refuse to do it, but bring resolution to conflict and give each other enough room for individuality and room to grow. Give each other the benefit of the doubt and do not judge each other's motives.

Communicate

There is a scripture that cuts across the grain of our understanding. According to Matt 5:14–16:

> You are the light of the world. A city on a hill cannot be hidden. Neither do people light a lamp and put it under a bowl. Instead they put it on its stand, and it gives light to everyone in the house. In the same way, let your light shine before men, that they may see your good deeds and praise your Father in heaven.

The Word tells us not to perform our works before men with the motive of self-glorification. But we must tell people what we have been up to, the struggles we have overcome and joy we have felt. We tell them not to brag, but to involve others in our story. People love stories well told, and every person you can interest in your Christ-like life is a person who can come out better because of it.

When you tell family and friends, even those who aren't Christian, of the drunken guy you helped get into recovery or that the guy who stole your lawnmower is back and repentant, it shows that people can grow and that anyone can help.

This is how the world around you will change. You will grow in influence to urge all people toward reconciliation with God through His son and toward this new life of sacrificial living. What the world has been missing is the Christian lifestyle! We will see incredible change as we apply ourselves.

RULES FOR CHRISTIAN RADICALS

When I'm using the word radical, I don't mean extremist or zealot. The Bible warns against fanaticism: "It is good to grasp the one and not let go of the other. The man who fears God will avoid all extremes" (Eccl 7:18).

We aren't extremists, but radicals in the classic sense—in the sense that we hold and are devoted to the roots of our faith, that we are devoted to love. God is love and His command is to love. What is more fundamental to our faithfulness to the Lord than to be true to love?

As radicals, we must restrict ourselves to the basics of theology. Our purpose is to bring His Kingdom to bear on the world around us. This ultimately means influencing people to bring them a new lifestyle.

In order to achieve this, we must have a strong theology of the gospel. Salvation occurs through faith in Jesus and will result in obedience of His command to love others. We must find those in need and help them. We must inspire those around us to this ultimate good and invite them to live as we have been shown.

This lifestyle will challenge the people in our lives to make the same change that has come to us.

Here is a description of the heart of a Christian Radical:

- Love goes
- Love sees
- Love hears
- Love understands and empathizes
- Love hopes
- Love says yes
- Love helps and gives
- Love suffers
- Love has no limits
- Love never gives up

OPERATION DELUGE

The mission of Operation Deluge, is to flood this country with activity minded followers of Jesus who will love without limit. We need Operation Deluge to reinforce our convictions, encourage us, and provide resources.

Operation Deluge was developed once I began writing this book. I realized that many of you will finish the book with the feeling that you want more. It wouldn't have been responsible of me to merely dump all this on you without providing you with a doable plan and without support in Operation Deluge.

The site has blogs, forums, and a library. There will also be Facebook entries and a weekly podcast. Visit the site once a week so you don't miss new content, and be encouraged and helped as we team up to create a transformation that lasts.

138

ABOUT THE AUTHOR

Cliff is a pastor and missionary. He lives with his wife and six children North of Seattle, Washington.

He studied engineering at Washington State University and worked as a nuclear engineer. After completing service in the Air Force National Guard, he and his family served street kids in Colombia, South America.

He, with a team of friends, have planted two churches in the Northwest. Cliff is currently helping the poor of the community in drug/alcohol rehab, housing, and career development.

He is also working on economic development in poor countries. All income generated by the sales of books goes to this work.

140

PURCHASE

You can purchase this book and other titles by Clifford E. Williams in the Kindle version or paperback from amazon.com. Check out his new book <u>The Venerators</u> also.